The Story of
My Life: Joseph

Kathy A. Weckwerth

Kathy A. Weckwerth

The Story of My Life: Joseph

A Women's 10 week Bible Study

Learning Life Lessons from Genesis

 The Story of My Life: Joseph is a ten week Bible study of the life of Joseph as found in Genesis 37-50. As we journey through the pages of Joseph's life and look at the snapshots taken from the camera lens of the Bible, we embrace the lessons he learned throughout his trials from *the pit* to *the prison* to *the palace.*

Using my personal real-life stories and experiences, along with Biblical truths, I will help you to discover valuable lessons through Joseph's journey by helping you determine how to trust God's faithfulness through your path and His promises.

The Story of My Life: Joseph
by Kathy A. Weckwerth

Published by Creative Days, Inc.
P.O. Box 73
Benson, Minnesota 56215

Cover Design: Peter Grossman
Layout Design: Marea Anderson
Editor: Susan C. Snow

Visit the author's website at www.KathyWeckwerth.com
Visit the author's ministry website at www.bestlifeministries.com

ISBN: 978-1-312-90630-3

To my wonderful Farmer Dean, who spends every day taking the snapshots of our lives and filling a scrapbook of fabulous days and nights that makes up our life together.
Thanks for making the story of my life have a better ending.

The Story of My Life: Joseph
Life Lessons from Genesis 37 - 50

The Story of My Life: Joseph 📷

*The purpose of life is not to be happy. It is to be useful,
to be honorable, to be compassionate, to have it make some
difference that you have lived and lived well.*

Ralph Waldo Emerson

My daddy used to tell me that God gave us the stories in the Bible so that we could learn from each situation. He would tell me that I could avoid trouble, embrace hope, and grow in faith, if I learned from the pages of the stories of their lives.

The story of my life is one mixed with vitality and fatigue, joy and trials, good and evil, and I am sure it is much like yours. But some pages in the book of my life are more difficult to read, and at times my heart would like to skip over those chapters, or completely tear the pages out of my book.

I vividly remember that hot August morning as I clutched the blankets on my bed tightly around me like a life preserver around my soul. Perhaps if I slept, just let myself keep sleeping, when I awakened it would all be a bad dream.

Unable to control the current that was dragging me under, I was propelled into a messy divorce. I could not breathe, I could not think, I could not help myself. Day after day, I went deeper into the pit of despair. My three children would awake each morning, come downstairs for breakfast as I greeted them in my old gray faded pajamas. It took every ounce of motherhood that I owned to produce a smile and a cheerful attitude that would feed them breakfast and then scoot them out the door to school.

As soon as they left I would find myself on the floor of the kitchen. Remaining in my old faded pajamas all day, I would be unable to think straight. The darkness would seep in and I would once again begin to recount what had taken place.

Betrayal and danger were stored down inside the story of my life, as I had been happily naive behind the camera lens living through each day. Those days and nights had flown by to equal almost twenty years of marriage, but each year zipped by without my cognizance of the treachery that was taking place, until the inevitable happened and truth, as it always does, floated to the surface to emit light throughout the murkiness of the images capturing my life.

A phone call from a detective at the local police station announced the drug scandal that was taking place between my husband and his friend. All the ugly pieces of the story were given to me, one by one, as my stomach turned, my heart ached, and the ever-present spirit of betrayal set into my soul.

Not only had I been betrayed by my spouse who was living a secret life, but the church where I worked stood strongly against divorce. They couldn't comprehend the danger we were in so they pressured me to stay married, and if I did not, they pushed for my resignation. I was flat on the floor of my kitchen, in the pit I called Hell, uncertain if I could get up to move, let alone uncertain of where my next steps would take me.

That specific morning I still remember vividly. I lay on the cool linoleum floor of my kitchen. A call came in from a woman who had heard about my circumstances. "Leave the church!" she screamed

into the phone. "Christians are all the same. They will never support you. They are meant to desert you in your time of need. I worked for a church and when my husband left me for another church member, the church fired me. Walk away, Kathy, just walk away. I stopped believing in God. You should join me."

In that moment in time I was faced with the greatest challenge of my life. Would I stay in that pit that I had been thrown into by another's bad choices, or would I stand up, get out, and keep going for God? With a deep breath, raw determination, and a shout out to God to save me, *I chose God*.

> There will be moments in our lives when we are faced with crisis, and the way that we determine who we will become, is by the choice we make in that moment.

There will be moments in our lives when we are faced with crisis, and the way that we determine who we will become, is by the choice we make in that moment.

There will be days and nights in your own life where you are propelled onto a path that you would have never taken if it was up to you alone. There will be places on the journey where you end up being cast into the pit of despair and wondering how you will ever get out. There will be moments in this life when you are faced with the critical choice of facing things with strong faith or turning and walking away.

But the comfort of being in the pit is that while we are there, the Lord never leaves us, and when we seek Him desperate for release, He sets us free! *"Out of my distress I called on the Lord; the Lord answered me and set me free"* Psalm 118:5 *(ESV)*.

The story of Joseph's life from *the pit*, to *the prison*, to *the palace*, is found in Genesis chapters 37-50 and delivers a chronicle of intrigue, jealousy, betrayal, courage, destiny, and reconciliation.

As we turn and open the pages of his story and begin to unfold the days and nights of his life, we will find ourselves back in the land of Canaan with his father, Jacob, and God's promise to this chosen leader.

Jacob was the son of Isaac and Rebekah, the grandson of Abraham. In Genesis 17, God makes a covenant with Abraham, Jacob's grandfather, and promised that he would be the father of many nations.

Look Up: Genesis 17:1-5

"When Abram was ninety-nine years old, the Lord appeared to him and said, 'I am God Almighty, walk before me and be blameless. I will confirm my covenant between me and you and will greatly increase your numbers.' Abram fell facedown, and God said to him, 'As for me, this is my covenant with you: You will be the father of many nations. No longer will you be called Abram, your name will be Abraham, for I have made you a father of many nations.'"

God is beginning the story of Joseph's life by making the covenant with Joseph's grandfather, Abraham. Many tribes and nations will come from Abraham, Isaac, and Jacob. This promise is once again reiterated between God and Joseph's father, Jacob, in Genesis 35.

Look Up: Genesis 35: 10-11

"God said to him, 'Your name is Jacob, but you will no longer be called Jacob; your name will be Israel.' So he named him Israel. And God said to him, 'I am God Almighty, be fruitful and increase in number. A nation and a community of nations will come from you, and kings will come from your body.'"

Jacob's twelve sons are the patriarchs of the twelve tribes of Israel. The sons of Israel are as follows: Reuben, Simeon, Levi, Judah, Issachar, Zebulun, *(sons that Leah bore)* Gad, and Asher *(sons that Leah's maidservant Zilpah bore)*. Dan, Naphtali *(sons that Rachel's maidservant Bilhah bore)* Joseph, Benjamin, *(sons that Rachel bore)*.

The lineage of Christ comes directly from these men, Abraham, Isaac, Jacob and Judah.

Look Up: Matthew 1:1-2

"A record of the genealogy of Jesus Christ the son of David, the son of Abraham: Abraham was the father of Isaac, Isaac the father of Jacob. Jacob the father of Judah and his brothers."

As we continue to peruse the genealogy of Jacob, and follow down through the years in the pages as the disciple Matthew records the lineage, we will see that such important Bible characters such as King David, King Solomon, King Jehoshaphat, and Joseph, the husband of Mary, are directly in the lineage of the Savior.

Look Up: Matthew 1:17

"Thus there were fourteen generations in all from Abraham to David, fourteen from David to the exile to Babylon, and fourteen from the exile to the Christ."

So often in scripture, God is teaching us life lessons through the pages of many Biblical character's stories. He weaves in and out the shortcomings, strong traits, and human flaws that we can learn from, and inspires and motivates us to emulate the good and learn from the bad.

As we prepare to open up the pages of the story of Joseph's life, it's important for us to understand how God draws parallels between

Joseph (*Yosef* in Hebrew) and Jesus (*Yeshua* in Hebrew).

① Both born through miracles

 Look Up: Genesis 30: 22-24 (Joseph)

"Then God remembered Rachel; He listened to her and enabled her to conceive. She became pregnant and gave birth to a son and said, 'God has taken away my disgrace.' She named him Joseph, and said, 'May the Lord add to me another son.'"

 Look Up: Matthew 1:18 (Jesus)

"This is how the birth of Jesus the Messiah came about: His mother Mary was pledged to be married to Joseph, but before they came together, she was found to be pregnant through the Holy Spirit."

② Both were shepherds

 Look Up: Genesis 37:2 (Joseph)

"This is the account of Jacob's family line. Joseph, a young man of seventeen, was tending the flocks with his brothers, the sons of Bilhah and the sons of Zilpah, his father's wives, and he brought their father a bad report about them."

 Look Up: John 10:14 (Jesus)

"I am the good shepherd; I know my sheep and my sheep know me."

③ Both suffered under others and their jealousy

 Look Up: Genesis 37:5 (Joseph)

"Joseph had a dream, and when he told it to his brothers, they hated him all the more."

Look Up: John 11:48 (Jesus)

"If we let him go on like this, everyone will believe in him, and then the Romans will come and take away both our temple and our nation."

④ Both were stripped of their coat

 Look Up: Genesis 37:23 (Joseph)

"So when Joseph came to his brothers, they stripped him of his robe--the ornate robe he was wearing ... "

 Look Up: John 19:23-24 (Jesus)

"When the soldiers crucified Jesus, they took his clothes, dividing them into four shares, one for each of them, with the undergarment remaining. This garment was seamless, woven in one piece from top to bottom. 'Let's not tear it,' they said to one another. 'Let's decide by lot who will get it.' This happened that the scripture might be fulfilled that said, 'They divided my clothes among them and cast lots for my garment.'"

⑤ Both were sold for pieces of silver

 Look Up: Genesis 37:28 (Joseph)

"So when the Midianite merchants came by, his brothers pulled Joseph up out of the cistern and sold him for twenty shekels of silver to the Ishmaelites, who took him to Egypt."

 Look Up: Matthew 26:15 (Jesus)

"' ... What are you willing to give me if I deliver him over to you?' So they counted out for him thirty pieces of silver."

⑥ Both were betrayed

Look Up: Genesis 39:16-18 (Joseph)

"She kept his cloak beside her until his master came home. Then she told him this story: 'That Hebrew slave you brought us came to me to make sport of me. But as soon as I screamed for help, he left his cloak beside me and ran out of the house.'"

Look Up: Matthew 26:48-49 (Jesus)

"Now the betrayer had arranged a signal with them: 'The one I kiss is the man; arrest him.' Going at once to Jesus, Judas said, 'Greetings, Rabbi!' and he kissed him."

⑦ Both gave God the glory for their abilities to predict the future

Look Up: Genesis 40:8 (Joseph)

"'We both had dreams,' they answered, 'but there is no one to interpret them.' Then Joseph said to them, 'Do not interpretations belong to God? Tell me your dreams.'"

Look Up: John 12:49 (Jesus)

"For I did not speak on my own, but the Father who sent me commanded me to say all that I have spoken."

⑧ Both were thirty years old when God started them in their ministry

Look Up: Genesis 41:46 (Joseph)

"Joseph was thirty years old when he entered the service of Pharaoh king of Egypt. And Joseph went out from Pharaoh's presence and traveled throughout Egypt."

📷 **Look Up: Luke 3:23a (Jesus)**

"Now Jesus himself was about thirty years old when he began his ministry ..."

⑨ **Both have a God-ordained purpose to fulfill that will save others**

📷 **Look Up: Genesis 41:55 (Joseph)**

"When all Egypt began to feel the famine, the people cried to Pharaoh for food. Then Pharaoh told all the Egyptians, 'Go to Joseph and do what he tells you.'"

📷 **Look Up: John 2:5 (Jesus)**

"His mother said to the servants, 'Do whatever he tells you.'"

⑩ **Both have three key points of service**

Joseph was thrown into the well *(the pit)* for three days, sold into slavery and then cast into *the prison* and finally became the leader of Pharaoh's land and *the palace*.

Jesus was thrown before the crowds and nailed to the cross *(the pit)*, buried in the tomb *(the prison)* and is seated at the right throne of the Father in Heaven *(the palace)* over a period of three days.

📷 **Look Up: Genesis 45:8 (Joseph)**

"So then, it was not you who sent me here, but God. He made me father to Pharaoh, lord of his entire household and ruler of all Egypt."

📷 **Look Up: Luke 24:7 (Jesus)**

"The Son of Man must be delivered over to the hands of sinners, be

crucified and on the third day be raised again."

⑪ Both remained faithful to God as Joseph saved the people from starvation and Jesus saved the people from their sins

Look Up: Genesis 45:11 (Joseph)

"I will provide for you there, because five years of famine are still to come. Otherwise you and your household and all who belong to you will become destitute."

Look Up: John 3:16 (Jesus)

"For God so loved the world that He gave His only begotten Son that whosoever believes in Him should not perish but have everlasting life" *(KJV).*

The story of Joseph's life is one that takes a seventeen year old boy and morphs him, shapes him, and matures him into someone who is used by God in such a mighty way, that his story affects the story of your life. Without Joseph's trials and tribulations, without God's work on developing His character and his skill set, the Israelites would have died and there would have been no brother, Judah, and his lineage, in which the Savior emerges. With each page turned, we walk with Joseph from *pit ... to prison ... to palace. We walk through his story and see his purpose.*

Everything that happened to Joseph was allowed by God for the good of Joseph and for the good of the bigger picture ... *the good of God's chosen people.*

The timing in each chapter of his story is God-orchestrated. First, we see *pain.* Next, we see *purpose.* Until finally, we see *a plan. God's plan.* God's in the business of taking what's broken, what's crushed, what's ruined, what's sitting in the bottom of a well, or laying on the floor of a prison cell, or the floor of a kitchen, and redeeming that life with purpose and meaning.

The story of your life is one that God has written and one that only you can share. What story is being written on the pages of your life? It will be one that God is writing, one that you will live out and read through, and one that will have great purpose. What will be the purpose of the story of your life? *"For I know the plans I have for you,' declares the Lord, 'plans to prosper you and not to harm you, plans to give you hope and a future'"* Jeremiah 29:11.

Questions:

1. God has a purpose for your life and yet life can become tedious if you do the same thing every day. What is the most difficult part of understanding whether or not your day in, day out, routine has any purpose? What steps could you take to change your life from feeling humdrum and uninspiring to seeing God's purpose and intention for your life?

2. Scripture says to wait patiently for the Lord and He will lift you out of the pit. Name a time when you felt like you were in a pit of despair. If you are trying to get out of the pit by yourself, do you find yourself slipping back in and are you tired of the struggle? What Godly action is needed to propel you out of the pit?

3. Do you feel that God has blessed you, or are you are feeling God has overlooked or deserted you? Which feeling is most often on your heart? How did you come to that conclusion?

4. Joseph dealt with the challenges of jealousy, adversity, betrayal, and bitterness. These same challenges ~ resentment, misfortune, disappointment and distress ~ may be causing pain in our lives. Explain which of these you are dealing with today.

📷 **Look Up:**

1. **Deuteronomy 31:6**

2. **Psalm 27:1**

3. **Isaiah 41:13**

4. **Philippians 4:6-7**

📷 **Songs:**

Hymn: "All the Way My Savior Leads Me" *(Fanny J. Crosby)*
Contemporary: "Our God" *(Chris Tomlin)*

📷 **Closing Prayer:**

Dear Jesus,

Thank you so much that my
life is not happenstance.

I praise You today
because You take away
my darkness, my loneliness,
my fear, and my hopelessness
that I feel in tough times

You embrace me
with your complete
comforting love.

The story of my life
chapter by chapter,
has always and will always
encompass a plan and a purpose

... Your plan and Your purpose.

In Jesus' Name, Amen.

CHAPTER 1
Jealousy 📷

The jealous are troublesome to others,
but a torment to themselves.

William Penn

📷 **Snapshot:** Last week we learned that God's plans are very different from ours, and when we think all hope is lost, we find that hope was never really lost at all. God has a purpose for our lives!

A chill ran up my spine as I realized what had just happened. Once again, the young store clerk who embraced a jealous spirit had won. I had lost and she had won. I felt disappointment and defeat running through my veins and stood silent to contemplate what had just happened to me.

The afternoon had arrived as it normally would. I was in high school at the time, and after school I would walk one mile to my job at a lovely jewelry store on the town square.

Two years earlier, I had been approached by the jewelry store's owner, Ruth, and asked if I wanted to work with her at her family-owned store. She was a dear friend of my mother and I was a dear friend of her mother.

Each week I walked to the nursing home behind my house and visited Ruth's eighty year old mother. The elderly woman was sweet and only spoke Swedish, but I loved her and she loved me. This created some favoritism in the heart of Ruth as she put me on staff at her jewelry store.

When I arrived on the job, her oldest son, Steve, welcomed me and took me under his wing. I found the work interesting, loved the customers, and enjoyed the beauty of the store and jewelry. I found favor in the heart of my boss, Steve *(many thanks to my mother's homemade cherry pies she would periodically bake for the store).*

But there was one downside to the job ... the dreaded co-worker, *Julie Ann.* Julie Ann was a few years older than me, had graduated and worked at the store as her sole position. Julie Ann had spent approximately six months dating my older brother and had already decided she neither liked me or my brother! Trouble began from the moment I was hired. Jealousy permeated from every corner of Julie Ann's persona.

Julie Ann scowled at me each time I arrived after school. I could not figure out what to do to change her attitude towards me. Nothing worked. Each day I would come in the store with a positive attitude, and each day I would walk out like a little puppy dog with my tail between my legs.

The afternoons when Ruth was gone and Steve was busy were the worst. Julie Ann would say, "Go clean all the shelves with crystal pieces."

I would politely answer, "But, Julie Ann, you had me clean the crystal two days ago."

Julie Ann responded, "So, they're dirty! Don't argue."

I would re-do the work I had previously completed. Cleaning all of the crystal was a nightmare of a job!

On and on the harsh attitude continued. The criticisms of my outfits, my hair style, and my mannerisms were never ceasing. Any difficult, gross, dirty and disgusting job was held off and given to me by Julie Ann, once I would arrive for work.

16

I remember one specific incident, Julie Ann had told me to vacuum the rugs, but Steve called me into his office. I gladly shut the vacuum cleaner off and headed in to see him. He told me about watches that needed to be mailed. Steve said, "Kathy, I only trust you with this task. I don't even trust myself! There are two watches that need to be mailed out. They are valued at over ten thousand dollars and one goes out east and one goes to Kansas City. Wrap each one separately and carefully. Take your time and don't mix them up. Do you hear me? Don't mix them up or I will be in the most horrific trouble I could ever imagine!"

I assured him I would do it immediately and then would make sure they went to the right owners. I looked them over, memorized the boxes with the correct name, and set them far apart on the back counter as I began to wrap them.

"Ding," the bell above the door rang to let us know that a customer had arrived at the front of the store. Julie Ann came back and barked the order, "Go take care of that customer." Then she saw what I was doing and a gleam shot out of her eye. "I'll finish this," she stated.

"But Julie Ann," I protested, "I was given strict orders that I was to do this for Steve. It's crucial nothing gets mixed up."

"Mixed up?" she questioned, "Of course not! I will finish this. Go take care of that couple immediately."

Sure enough, when I finished with the customers, the boxes were ready for the mail. Julie Ann acted like a cat with a mouse in her mouth, and I fought the temptation to

> If jealousy is not kept in check and quickly removed from our hearts, it will continue to progress to a deeper level and take the next step.

open the boxes. I couldn't imagine that her jealousy would lead her to such a horrific task.

One week later, I was called into the office where Steve chewed me out. I explained that I had not wrapped them and got into more trouble. Jealous Julie Ann came in and denied ever wrapping them and said I had done the work, I had mixed them up, and I was to blame. "She's not so perfect, is she?" Julie Ann questioned as she deliberately discredited me.

Desperately I wanted to defend myself. I bit my lip, walked out of the store and ran home. I cried and told Mom I would never go back. Then my mother said something so profound that I never forgot it. She said, "At times we will want to turn and run when things don't go our way. But it's in those times that we are made stronger, that our character is built, and our faith in God becomes deeper. Let's pray and trust God to figure this all out. Kathy, go back in there tomorrow with a smile on your face, a great attitude in your spirit, and work as hard as you can. That is what will continue to convince them that you are not defeated by trickery and malice. You will not be taken down by jealousy, but you will meet it head on and rise above it."

I went back the next day, and I did feel a little awkward around the staff, but I continued to work hard and to pray and focus on everything good. Julie Ann ignored me. Jealousy had not won that day. I thought it did, but I closed the book on jealousy, trusted God, and focused on the next page in the book of my life.

Jealousy is such an ugly sin. We have all embraced it and been jealous of others. We have all experienced others being jealous of us. Sometimes we portray it as a fun and silly expression, teasing that we would love that friend's new car or great job. But the old saying that "many a truth

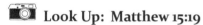

is said in jest," stands true in most circumstances. We really do want that car and we would love that great job. We are thrust into a sinful mentality.

If jealousy is not kept in check and quickly removed from our hearts, it will continue to progress to a deeper level and take its next step. That next step is action.

First, we conceive the desire in our ***heart,*** *I want that.*

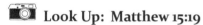 **Look Up: Matthew 15:19**

"For out of our hearts come evil thoughts ..."

Next, we say with our ***mouth,*** *"I wish that was mine."*

Look Up: Luke 6:45b

"For out of the overflow of his heart his mouth speaks."

And finally, if not kept in check and controlled, we move to ***action*** and hurting someone because they have what we want.

That hurt can be as simple as cutting words, shunning someone, treating others with disrespect, or having an all-out verbal fight. At times, we will see the worst part of jealousy in individuals who have committed horrible acts of violence and crimes of jealousy will be reported in the news.

Webster's Dictionary states that *jealousy* means *"hostile toward a rival or one believed to enjoy an advantage."*

In Genesis 37, we see that our character, Joseph, begins his story with ten brothers who are jealous of him *(there are twelve brothers total, but baby brother, Benjamin, is not involved in this part of the story).*

Sometimes that old spirit of jealousy continues throughout the pages of a family's history. When we look at Joseph's ancestors, it is very clear that jealousy did not just begin with Jacob's twelve children, but had a beginning much earlier with Jacob himself in how he dealt with his brother, Esau, and their grandfather, Isaac.

Isaac has twin sons, Jacob *(Joseph's father)* and Esau. Esau is the oldest brother who is to receive the coveted birthright. One day, he is so hungry that he sells that birthright for some stew that his brother Jacob serves him *(Genesis 25:31-34)*. This sets jealousy and hatred ablaze in the heart of Esau towards brother Jacob.

Since Esau is the firstborn who deserves his father's blessing, Isaac calls for Esau to deliver that blessing but their mother Rebekah schemes with her son, Jacob, to go in his place and tricks Isaac into delivering the blessing to Jacob, which was rightfully meant for Esau *(Genesis 27:1-40)*.

Twin feuding brothers and a very jealous, Esau, deliver a sad story. When Esau finds out that Jacob has received Esau's rightful blessing, his jealousy skips from *conceiving* the desire to hurt Jacob, to *saying* it out loud, to *wanting to act* on it.

Look Up: Genesis 27:41
"Esau held a grudge against Jacob because of the blessing his father had given him ... I will kill my brother Jacob."

The ancestry now portrays a strong thread of jealousy that connects page to page. But this family's history of jealousy moves to the next generation. Jacob has tricked his brother out of his birthright and his father's blessing, but now watch and see how he becomes tricked as his story unfolds.

Years go by and Jacob wants to marry the love of his life, Rachel. He offers Rachel's father seven years of labor in exchange for marriage to her *(Genesis 29:18)*. On their wedding night, Rachel's father sends his oldest daughter, Leah, to Jacob instead of Rachel. In the morning he discovers what has happened and realizes he has now been tricked *(sometimes life does the turn-about where one gets what one dishes out)* into marrying Leah, but he doesn't love Leah *(Genesis 29:17," Leah had weak eyes, but Rachel was lovely in form and beautiful")*. The threads of jealousy are now on both sides of the family ... between Joseph's father with his brother, and between his mother Rachel with her sister Leah. The saga of jealousy continues as the two sisters race to see which one of them can produce the most male offspring for Jacob.

📷 **Look Up: Genesis 30:1**

"When Rachel saw that she was not bearing Jacob any children, she became jealous of her sister. So she said to Jacob, 'Give me children, or I'll die!'"

Jealousy is in the inkwell that writes the pages of this part of the story. Finally, Joseph's mother, Rachel, becomes pregnant with Jacob's eleventh son, delivers him, and names him Joseph ... meaning, *"God adds."* Rachel dies while giving birth to Jacob's twelfth son, Benjamin. Jealousy is a human condition. John Ortberg says in one of his sermons, *"Time Magazine had a big cover story this week about siblings--about families. In it, they cited a lot of research. One was a study about fighting among siblings. Do you know how much fighting goes on among siblings? Kids between the ages of two and four average 6.2 fights an hour. That's about 90 fights a day. That's about 3000 fights per year!"*

As we turn the pages of the story, we see a warm spring day where a seventeen year old, Joseph, and his family were living in Canaan. The sons are out in the fields taking care of their flocks of sheep.

Joseph is the favored one. He's the babied one. Scripture tells us he is loved more than any of the other sons. Jacob gives him a special robe. The King James Bible informs us that it is a coat of many colors. Back then normal work clothes were bland and boring, so this colorful coat represents a position of honor and esteem. Wearing this coat probably excused Joseph from some jobs so that the coat wouldn't get ruined.

Now, can you imagine being one of twelve children and there is one robe and it is fantastic looking. It's a Ralph Lauren or a Kenneth Cole coat. You're thinking, *Wow, I'd look good in that coat. But Daddy's favorite gets it.* Insert jealousy ... *again.*

📷 **Look Up: Genesis 37:4**
"When his brothers saw that their father loved him more than any of them, they hated him and could not speak a kind word to him."

Joseph isn't just a good looking, well dressed young man, but he's also a bit of a tattle tale. He brings a bad report to Jacob about the brothers. Add on top of that, the already-have-it-jealousy and now the fact that Joseph is dreaming and reporting to his father and brothers about his dreams, and those dreams indicate that the family will eventually bow down to him, doesn't make him well-liked with his brothers. Interesting fact, dreams in those days were considered prophetic.

📷 **Look Up: Genesis 37:5**
"Joseph had a dream and when he told it to his brothers, they hated him all the more. He said to them, 'Listen to this dream I had. We were binding sheaves of grain out in the field when suddenly my sheaf rose and stood upright; while your sheaves gathered around mine and bowed down to it.'"

Sharing that dream with the already jealous brothers was a bad idea, as the jealousy stirs hatred into their hearts.

Look Up: Genesis 37:8

"'Do you intend to reign over us? Will you actually rule us?' And they hated him all the more because of his dream and what he had said."

Joseph once again relays to his siblings yet another dream that he has had only to make the brothers and his father upset.

Look Up: Genesis 37:9

"Then he had another dream, and he told it to his brothers. 'Listen,' he said. 'I had another dream, and this time the sun and moon and eleven stars were bowing down to me.'"

Joseph is adding insult to injury. Very often I asked myself why he would tell them one dream, let alone two. I always come back to the same answer: It was God's plan.

Theologians report Joseph as a boastful, naive seventeen-year-old kid, who was very prideful. Perhaps he was, but I like to think that he was excited about the dreams he was having and wanted to share them. God's plan all along was in Joseph sharing the dreams because this is the beginning of the story. God always connects the strands of time throughout our lives and weaves important things in and out of our days and nights. It was crucial that the brothers and Jacob all heard the prophetic dreams. Why? Because God will reveal Himself through them, in His own perfect time, and then we will see how God makes himself real in Joseph's story and the importance of the dreams at the end of the story. But for now, we will see how jealousy rules our emotions and can change the course of our lives and the lives of others.

American film director, Oliver Stone, says, *"Never underestimate the power of jealousy and the power of envy to destroy. Never underestimate that."*

It was bad enough for the half brothers to know that they were not as valued as Joseph, but now Joseph is rubbing it in, like salt to a wound. You would think Joseph would be respectful of his status and theirs, but he is only seventeen. They are thinking, *Enough!* The treasured kid with the Macy's coat gets his way all the time. The desire to respond to feelings of jealousy is *conceived*, the *words come out*, and the *action is taken*.

Even Joseph's father Jacob rebuked him because of his dream, asking Joseph if even his mother and father needed to bow themselves to the ground before him. Jacob sends Joseph to see if all was well with his brothers and the flocks. Joseph searches for his brothers at Shechem, but finds them near Dothan. Their jealousy is ruling their hearts and before Joseph reaches them, they are plotting to kill him. One brother alone, Reuben, tries to rescue him from death.

📷 Look Up: Genesis 37:22

"'Don't shed any blood. Throw him into this cistern (well or pit) here in the desert, but don't lay a hand on him.'"

When Joseph walks up to the ten brothers, they attack him and strip him of the lovely coat. He is cast into the cistern or a pit. Christian author and speaker, Beth Moore describes it as this: *"To the ancient Hebrew, a pit was a literal or figurative reference to the grave-to its threat-or to an abyss so deep the dweller within it felt like the living dead."* Joseph's brothers have thrown him in the bottom of a dry well.

The plot thickens when brother Judah decides that killing him is not quite the best punishment. Perhaps there is a moment of weakness in Judah's heart.

Look Up: Genesis 37:27
"'Come, let's sell him to the Ishmaelites and not lay our hands on him; after all, he is our brother, our own flesh and blood.' His brothers agreed."

Sold into slavery, for a mere twenty shekels of silver (about 8 ounces), to a caravan of Ishmaelites on their way from Gilead with merchandise to sell in Egypt, all to quench the emotion of the green-eyed giant, Jealousy.

As the brothers make their way back to their father Jacob, the prized ornate robe is now soaked in goat's blood by the brothers in hopes to cover up their sin. Out of the corner of their hearts, where the jealousy has grown leaps and bounds, they move forward to the next step of what happens when we act upon jealousy. There are always more steps. The next step will be to lie and cover up their actions, then to try to soothe their own conscience, and finally to try to forget Joseph ever existed.

Look Up: Genesis 37:31
"...We found this. Examine it to see whether it is your son's robe."

Notice that their jealousy, their anger, their rage, their you-deserved-it attitude has suddenly taken yet another step? Now, the brothers are detaching themselves from Joseph by saying, *"your son's robe."* Notice that they don't say, "our brother's robe." No, that's too close to home. That would remind them that they have sinned greatly against their own brother. Take two steps back and find yourself separate from the crime. Cover it up quickly. Think fast because you don't want to be responsible for your sin. Jacob mourns, as the pain is so deep.

Joseph's life is about to change forever, and the history of his pages, and the storyline of yours will be connected as we move forward and see that those who purchased Joseph have now sold Joseph to his destiny. Potiphar, one of Pharaoh's officials, the captain of the guard is now the proud owner of Joseph, the man who once his daddy's favorite, his mother's blessed, and the one who owned the special coat of many colors.

Author Shannon L. Alder writes, *"I am convinced that the jealous, the angry, the bitter and the egotistical are the first to race to the top of mountains. A confident person enjoys the journey, the people they meet along the way and sees life not as a competition. They reach the summit last because they know God isn't at the top waiting for them. He is down below helping his followers to understand that the view is glorious where ever you stand."*

When we are in a place where we are jabbed, ridiculed, mistreated, and laughed at, it's the norm to wonder what's wrong with us. But instead, God calls us to pray for those who hate us. How much easier is it to hate those people who are mean, and love those who support us and foster our uniqueness? God is always about the heart and He knows that the way to combat those ugly days of jealousy, is to be in prayer for those who are jealous. Quality people doing quality things attract jealous hearts that want that same quality for their life. Just think! All they'd really have to do is to begin to work with God on their own personalities and they'd be better themselves!

If you are experiencing bouts of jealousy towards others, it is time to ask God for help and forgiveness, and it is time to start working on controlling that emotion. My daddy always told me, "Kathleen, there will always be others who are miles ahead of you. **Learn from them.** There will always be others who are even with you. **Support them.** There will always be others who are miles behind you. **Cheer them on** in their endeavors. Always be content with who God's made you to be and know that you are never too old to learn."

Here are some steps to help you with others who are jealous of you.

📷 **STEP ONE:** *Understand* ~ that this is a battle every human encounters.

📷 **James 3:16,** *"For where jealousy and selfish ambition exist, there will be disorder and every vile practice" (ESV).*

📷 **James 4:1-2,** *"What causes quarrels and what causes fights among you? Is it not this, that your passions are at war within you? You desire and do not have, so you murder. You covet and cannot obtain, so you fight and quarrel. You do not have, because you do not ask" (ESV).*

📷 **Proverbs 27:4,** *"Wrath is cruel, anger is overwhelming, but who can stand before jealousy?" (ESV).*

📷 **STEP TWO:** *Remain patient* ~ towards the person who is jealous.

📷 **Philippians 2:3,** *"Do nothing from selfish ambition or conceit, but in humility count others more significant than yourselves" (ESV).*

📷 **Proverbs 14:30,** *"A heart at peace gives life to the body, but envy rots the bones."*

Galatians 5:22-23, *"But the fruit of the Spirit is love, joy, peace, patience, kindness, goodness, faithfulness, gentleness, self-control; against such things there is no law" (ESV).*

STEP THREE: *Embrace a loving attitude and pray* ~ for the person who is jealous.

Colossians 3:12-13, *"Put on then, as God's chosen ones, holy and beloved, compassionate hearts, kindness, humility, meekness, and patience, bearing with one another and, if one has a complaint against another, forgiving each other; as the Lord has forgiven you, so you also must forgive" (ESV).*

Ephesians 4:1-3, *"I therefore, a prisoner for the Lord, urge you to walk in a manner worthy of the calling to which you have been called, with all humility and gentleness, with patience, bearing with one another in love, eager to maintain the unity of the Spirit in the bond of peace" (ESV).*

John 13:35, *"By this all people will know that you are my disciples, if you have love for one another" (ESV).*

STEP FOUR: *Foster a humble spirit* ~ so you do not become jealous.

Psalm 25:9, *"He leads the humble in what is right, and teaches the humble His way" (ESV).*

I Peter 5:5, *"Likewise, you who are younger, be subject to the elders. Clothe yourselves, all of you, with humility toward one another, for "'God opposes the proud but gives grace to the humble'" (ESV).*

📷 **Psalm 149:4,** *"For the Lord takes pleasure in his people; he adorns the humble with salvation" (ESV).*

📷 **Steps Recapped:**

1. Understand ~ that this is a battle every human encounters.

2. Remain patient ~ towards the person who is jealous.

3. Embrace a loving attitude and pray ~ for the person who is jealous.

4. Foster a humble spirit ~ so you do not become jealous.

Jealousy is something we will face within ourselves and within others. It is inevitable. How we respond to it, how we learn and grow from it, and how we move past it, is the key to finding God's plan and purpose.

Throughout my own pages, I have long-since learned from those days at the jewelry store, that people who push you down are jealous and insecure.

📷 **Zoom In:** Joseph's family has had some issues in their past with jealousy. When Joseph's mother Rachel, delivers Joseph, his father Jacob is so grateful for him that he favors him above the other children. This creates deep resentment and grave jealousy towards Joseph. When God gives Joseph prophetic dreams that include what will happen to his family, Joseph shares them with his family and creates more animosity. When Joseph is sent out to find his brothers, they are plotting to kill him, but end up throwing him in a well *(pit)*. Joseph is then pulled out of *the pit* by his brothers and sold to traveling Ishmaelites for twenty shekels.

Life Lesson Learned: As I look back through my own story, I realize that I have been propelled to a better place from those who had a jealous attitude towards me. Each time someone criticized me or displayed jealousy, I became stronger *(once I dealt with the hurt and pain)*. I have learned that our job is to remain humble, to not provoke others to become jealous, to not become jealous over others, and to be an example of Christ. After all, closing the book on jealousy and not letting its pages rule over you is a great thing. You look out in freedom and you find that God is right next to you.

Questions:

1. In addition to giving a special coat to Joseph, do you believe Jacob was wrong in loving Joseph more than all his other sons? In your own family, do you feel that one relative receives or gives preferential treatment? Is there a Godly way to improve your relationship with this person?

2. Scripture tells the brothers were jealous when Joseph tells them about a dream where they will bow down to him. Could Joseph have avoided trouble if he didn't share his dreams? Why do you think Joseph revealed his dreams? Why was it important that Joseph knew he was created for a divine purpose?

3. Share a time when you were ridiculed, mistreated, and laughed at because of someone's jealousy? How did you respond to their jealousy? Did you feel powerless, inferior and insecure? Were you hurt and resentful or did you focus on your strong points? Did you fight back or were you nice to them? Did you pray for them?

4. Give an example of a circumstance where you were jealous of someone else. Did you act on that jealousy? What was the outcome? What helped you understand the root of the jealousy? Were you able to find it in your heart to believe in your own abilities, let go of the jealousy and move forward?

📷 **Look Up:**

1. **Exodus 20:17**

2. **Romans 5:1-5**

3. **Romans 12:2**

4. **I Corinthians 3:3**

📷 **Songs:**

Hymn: "Grace Greater Than Our Sin" *(Julia Johnston and Daniel Towner)*
Contemporary: "You Are My King" *(Billy Foote)*

Closing Prayer:

Dear Jesus,
I know there will be times
when I look at others
with a jealous heart.

Please forgive me and help me
to be thankful and grateful
for all You've given me.

Help me to love those
who are jealous of me,
to forgive them for any hurt
that their jealousy may cause.

Help me to be a reflection
of Your love, Your grace,
and Your kindness.

In Jesus' name, Amen.

CHAPTER 2
Adversity 📷

*Comfort and prosperity have never enriched
the world as much as adversity has.*

Billy Graham

📷 **Snapshot:** Last week we learned that other people's jealousy and actions will sometimes have an adverse affect on our lives, but we are not to fear, because God is always in control!

It seems to be a given. No matter what you do, there is always trouble. The car breaks down, the lawn mower won't work, your boss has the flu and you become infected, the telephone company has mistakenly billed you $1000.00 instead of $100.00, your dog ran away, your friend is mad at you ... on and on the days tick by that make up the story of your life.

I still remember one particular day I felt troubled and the problems seemed insurmountable, while the clock of life kept ticking.

I was in the middle of a struggle at my job. At that time, I was a worship director at a local church, and a husband and wife were creating enormous amounts of static for me, our staff, and our worship team.

Although they were thirty-something, it didn't make any difference in how they were acting. My pastor and I met over and over to try to calm the waters and nothing would appease them. I remember the nasty letter that they wrote to me. They didn't like my style, they didn't like my song choices, and it boiled down to the fact that they very unhappy.

The trouble began increasing, the emails were flying, the phone was ringing, and now I received an unkind letter from another couple stating that they would leave church if the troublesome couple were to quit the team.

That was it! I couldn't take it another minute and I ran to my closet and crouched in the corner.

In order to understand my odd behavior, you must understand the pages that make up my own story. As a seven-year-old vacationing at Grandma Thelma's each summer, I would look at my great grandmother Louisa's dresser. It was lovely. Made out of sturdy oak, with lovely brass handles, the top of the dresser featured beautiful side drawers that held hankies. Great Aunt Edie had painted it yellow, pink, and finally the white that it stayed.

My Grandma stated the words that I would treasure my whole life. "Kathy, I know my mother would have loved for you to have this dresser. Someday, it will come to live with you!" And so it did. After Grandma passed away, and Cousin Cindy was done with it, it came to be in my closet, where each day I would use it and remember the strong faith of my grandmothers. Today, I needed to emulate that faith in God.

Crouched underneath the hangers of sweaters brushing against my forehead, I began to cry and then pray. I heard the door open and Farmer Dean *(my husband's also a farmer)* opened the door and quietly said, "Ma'am? Whatcha doin'?"

"Hiding," I answered.

"From what?" he asked.

"Trouble," I sighed.

He gently sat on the side of the bed slowly putting on his shoes and said, "I have some bad news for you ... I think it's still going to find you."

He headed outside to mow the lawn while I hid in the corner moping a bit.

"Why? Why?" I asked God. "Why does it seem like there are always several awful things happening in my life at the same time?"

And then it happened. Just like that it hit me. I felt that still, small voice of the Holy Spirit asking, "Kathy, what do your favorite Bible characters have in common?" I smiled as I recited them out loud:

Noah and the ark

> *... a lot of rain*

Abraham and Isaac

> *... a big sacrifice*

Moses and the Israelites

> *... lost in the desert*

Queen Esther and King Xerxes

> *... a kingdom rule*

Daniel and the lion's den

> *... a big hungry lion*

Jonah and the large fish

> *... darkness in a belly*

Mary having a baby

... virgin having God's Son

Jesus' disciples out in the storm

... a big storm

Stephen and the stoning

... persecuted for faith

Paul and Silas in a prison cell

... prisoner for faith

And most importantly

Jesus and the cross

... our Savior dying

What did they have in common? Trouble! The people we read about in our quiet times struggled just like we do. Quite honestly, they had it a lot harder than we do. Yet, we all have one thing in common ... when trouble comes, God is with us. We don't walk through the trials alone ... not ever.

In the corner of the closet that day, I took some time to pray. I laid every single concern, email, letter, discussion, criticism, and future problem at the foot of the cross. I rejoiced as I thought about the list of Bible characters who had suffered for Christ's sake and had the tenacity to walk through problems. They kept going. They did not hide in their closets. Well, Jonah was trying to run and hide, but that's another story.

I stood up, took a deep breath, and got back to work. My husband came in peering over my shoulder as I continued working, and said to me, "There's a knock at the door. Should I get it?"

"Who's there?" I smiled.

"Trouble," he answered.

"I'm not surprised. But this time, I'm not hiding."

Webster's Dictionary says that the word *adversity* means *"a state or instance of serious or continued difficulty or misfortune."*

> ... when trouble comes, God is with us We don't walk through the trials alone ... not ever.

Joseph certainly falls under that description. As a matter of fact, in Genesis 39, where we see the story unfolding for Joseph, it seems fair to think that if we looked up the word *adversity* in the dictionary, we'd see a photo of Joseph! Trouble, trouble, trouble.

Years ago, I heard Dr. James Dobson on his talk show, *Focus on the Family,* talking about trouble. I remember him saying that normal life will give you trouble, and then you may get a reprieve for about two weeks, and then trouble shows up again. I am sure Joseph was waiting for the two weeks to come without problems!

We learned in our last chapter that Joseph had been sold for twenty shekels of silver to some Ishmaelites on their way to Egypt. Once in Egypt, he is now sold to one of Pharaoh's main leaders, Potiphar.

Look Up: Genesis 39:1

"Now Joseph had been taken down to Egypt. Potiphar, an Egyptian who was one of Pharaoh's officials, the captain of the guard, bought him from the Ishmaelites who had taken him there."

He has already been stripped of the royalty of a beautiful multi-colored robe, and now he finds himself in the corner of the bottom of *the pit.*

His only hope ... *God.*

The story of Joseph tells us repeatedly that *"The Lord was with Joseph"* (Genesis 39:2-3; 39:20-21 and 39:23). Through the trials, through the troubles, through the adversity, God has never left Joseph.

Scripture tells us that when we live on planet earth, we will have adversity. Plan on it. But the greatest encouragement we will ever have is that we are never alone. God does not leave us in our time of need. At times, He allows the troubles to come because in those troubles we find that we grow, that we become better, and our faith becomes stronger. Our character becomes deeper and we learn things that we would have never learned if life was just peaceful without any strife. But He never leaves us!

If we think about remaining stationary all time, without any challenge or trials, we become complacent. When we experience hardship, it can propel us into finding answers and determining steps to change the situation. This leads to growth in our character and in our ability to help others when they have problems. Listen to what God says to Isaiah:

Look Up: Isaiah 43:2

"When you go through deep waters, I will be with you. When you go through rivers of difficulty, you will not drown. When you walk through the fire of oppression, you will not be burned up; the flames will not consume you."

Although Joseph is a slave now and freedom has escaped him, the Lord made Joseph to prosper and he has the privilege of living in the same house as the Egyptian official, Potiphar. The Hebrew text uses the word *saris* to describe Potiphar, meaning *"someone who belongs to the king"* or *"captain of the guard."* Potiphar trusts Joseph completely. As a slave, Joseph had no rights, yet Joseph proved himself to be a faithful servant.

Look Up: Genesis 39:4

"Joseph found favor in his eyes and became his attendant. Potiphar put him in charge of his household, and he entrusted to his care everything he owned."

The Lord does not bless Joseph alone, but he includes the blessing to Potiphar and everything in Potiphar's life. No wonder Joseph is completely trusted. Potiphar relaxed in his job without any concerns.

Look Up: Genesis 39: 5-6

"From the time he put him in charge of his household and of all that he owned, the Lord blessed the household of the Egyptian because of Joseph. The blessing of the Lord was on everything Potiphar had, both in the house and in the field. So he left in Joseph's care everything he had; with Joseph in charge, he did not concern himself with anything except the food he ate."

Life cannot stay the same as we turn the pages of the story and see that even though things are going well for Joseph, once again, adversity strikes.

Have you ever felt like you were in the corner of the closet? Perhaps in the corner of the pit? You were down and out, cast aside, fighting and worrying as you wonder how you'll ever get out of the trouble you are in, feeling like you are almost completely defeated. Notice I said, "Almost."

Somehow you get out of the trouble, or it is subdued, and things start looking better. You get to your three days or two week reprieve. You take a quick breath, and then the next tribulation hits. When we zoom in on the picture, we can only see a small piece of that picture, but God sees the big picture ... in its entirety.

Walt Disney says, *"All the adversity I've had in my life, all my troubles and obstacles, have strengthened me ... You may not realize it when it happens, but a kick in the teeth may be the best thing in the world for you."*

What Joseph doesn't know is this ... he is headed for a lot more turmoil and adversity. But the most wonderful thing that we learn about Joseph, through his story, is that he is not complaining, or throwing a tantrum. No, it is going to be the best thing in the world for him, and for everyone else. He remains level headed and continues strong in his faith. He does not question God; he just does his best in every situation.

Enter into the storyline, Potiphar's wife. She is given no name in the story. Perhaps because she is not important enough or perhaps because we are to focus on what happened when temptation came Joseph's way. Nevertheless, we read of no children born to Potiphar and his wife, and we know that he lives in a wealthy household, as he is an official to Pharaoh. The wife is obviously bored with her wealth and status, unhappy in her marriage, and thinks the handsome Joseph is the perfect solution to all of her troubles. She tries desperately to seduce him.

Scripture says Joseph is a handsome young man. Perhaps he looks like George Clooney or Brad Pitt. Since I'm an old movie buff, I imagine Joseph is a Gregory Peck look alike.

Look Up: Genesis 39:6b-7

"Now Joseph was well-built and handsome, and after a while his master's wife took notice of Joseph and said, 'Come to bed with me!'"

Temptation is there. I believe this is a man's greatest temptation and it is right in front of Joseph. I love the fact that Joseph says, "No." Because Potiphar has entrusted everything to Joseph, he will not betray him.

But Joseph takes it to a deeper level, and we see his faith in God and his devotion to the Almighty. Joseph says he will not betray Potiphar OR God. Likewise, Potiphar (who doesn't worship God but worships idols), recognizes God's presence in Joseph's life and trusts him because of it. Joseph has the guts to say, "No!"

 Look Up: Genesis 39:9b

"How then could I do such a wicked thing and sin against God?"

Wouldn't it have been nice if she would have just gotten that message? Okay, so Joseph isn't interested. I'll walk away. But, no, scripture says she has tenacity. He must have been really attractive and a dire temptation to her or she was looking towards this conquest to make her feel better about herself because day after day she is after Joseph to give in to her seductions.

 Look Up: Genesis 39:10

"And though she spoke to Joseph day after day, he refused to go to bed with her or even be with her."

Until one day, she pressures him and catches him by his cloak. He leaves his cloak and runs out of the house. Knock, knock, knock ... adversity is at Joseph's door, yet once again.

What happens when humans don't get what they want? Sometimes they act on resentment, bitterness, envy, or control. That's what Potiphar's wife did. She couldn't have what she wanted, so she threw a little tantrum and got Joseph in trouble with her husband. She goes before her husband and delivers her lie.

📷 Look Up: Genesis 39:14b-15

"He came in here to sleep with me, but I screamed. When he heard me scream for help, he left his cloak beside me and ran out of the house."

History tells us that Egyptian clothes worn by men were *"tunics made of linen with fringes hanging about the legs, called calasiris, and loose white woolen cloaks over these."*

Perhaps it was the white woolen cloak that was pulled, but the bottom line is that Joseph ran. He chose to do the right thing. Now, he will be punished by his master, Potiphar.

📷 Look Up: Genesis 39:19-20

"When his master heard the story his wife told him, saying 'this is how your slave treated me,' he burned with anger. Joseph's master took him and put him in prison, the place where the king's prisoners were confined."

At this point if I were Joseph, I'd be feeling really upset. Personally, I would want to defend myself and argue the points. But we see no chance of that happening for Joseph.

Potiphar's wife has crafted a huge lie. She was certainly hoping that Joseph would be killed, but Potiphar was in a tough place. Not only had he trusted Joseph with everything, but he knew that God was behind all of the blessings they had received. Most theologians believe that Potiphar's wife had a reputation for this kind of behavior, so the sentence was lighter for Joseph than it should have been. The lie was delivered. The lie took life. The lie changed a life.

Potiphar's wife's lie reminds me of something that happened several years ago. I told the story of my betrayal by my spouse at a women's retreat. When my talk was over, a couple of my staff greeted women at the door. A woman told my staff that my story about my life was a lie. She had attended my church, said it wasn't true, and was adamant that I should not continue with my ministry.

I was flabbergasted when I heard what had happened. The first thing I thought was how a stranger could possibly know what had happened to me. Was she there during the abuse? Was she there listening to what the police reported? The retreat workshop that I taught was a small crowd of about 15 women. I saw every face in that room for one hour. I didn't know any of them. And yet, this woman said she knew me and everything that I had told, in her mind, was an untruth.

When I told the story of what happened at the retreat to my friend, Todd, he said, "Kathy, there are times when people take truth and try to make it their own. That woman could have stood out in front of McDonald's down the road from you, and screamed, 'This is my McDonald's, I own this store,' and it wouldn't make it true. No matter how much she screams that it is the truth, it will never make it so."

Truth was just that ... truth. It could not be stretched or changed; it was just the plain, honest truth. Joseph knows what happened. Potiphar's wife knows what happened. God knows what happened. Nevertheless, off Joseph goes to prison for something he didn't do. Lies, trouble, adversity set in once again. We saw Joseph as a happy seventeen-year-old shepherding his flock, then as a sad young man thrown into a pit and sold as a slave. Next we saw him happily walking the floors of Pharaoh's officials in lovely freedom, while shortly after that he is sadly thrown into prison. The ups and downs of everyday life and adversity are quite evident in Joseph's storyline.

Whether Joseph is facing triumphs or trials, we see the wonderful comforting words of scripture, *"But while Joseph was there in the prison, the Lord was with him ...*" (Genesis 39:20b).

Joseph has passed this test. We know that he has been in the corner of the pit and we heard no complaints. We see that he has been thrown before his master and he has not betrayed God. Now, he will be cast into the prison. And yet ... not a doubt, not a word, not a fist shaking up to the heavens saying, "God, why did you allow this?" Joseph remains faithful and God remains with Joseph.

Joseph will head from the floor of *the pit*, to the floor of *the prison*. I'm sure he wondered where the purpose was, where the plan was, and where the point of everything would end up, but we know the end of the story and God has a plan!

William Shakespeare says of adversity, *"Let me embrace thee, sour adversity, for wise man say it is the wisest course."* It was a wise course because it is the next step that God has planned for Joseph.

God has given favor to Joseph in the house of Potiphar and God is with him. Now God showed Joseph kindness and granted him favor in the eyes of the prison warden. Joseph is now in charge of all those held in the prison. A young man never trained to be anything but a shepherd, once again is in a major leadership role. Over these years of being in charge of Potiphar's household, his untapped skills were being polished. Now, he will be in charge of the prison and his leadership will once again be polished because God will need Joseph to be a strong leader for many people in the next few years. And we wonder why we must go through adversity?

Look Up: Genesis 39:23

"The warden paid no attention to anything under Joseph's care, because the Lord was with Joseph and gave him success in whatever he did."

If you are in a place in your own personal story where life is difficult and you are wondering if God still cares about you, here are some steps I recommend that you implement to help maneuver you through the daily life.

STEP ONE: *Believe that no matter what the circumstances~* God is with you.

Psalm 91:14-15, *"'Because he loves me,' says the Lord, 'I will rescue him; I will protect him, for he acknowledges my name. He will call upon me, and I will answer him; I will be with him in trouble, I will deliver him and honor him.'"*

Isaiah 41:10, *"So do not fear, for I am with you; do not be dismayed for I am your God. I will strengthen you and help you; I will uphold you with my righteous right hand."*

Hebrews 13:5, *"Never will I leave you; never will I forsake you."*

STEP TWO: *Take control over your emotions* ~ remain calm and faithful.

James 1:4, *"Perseverance must finish its work so that you may be mature and complete not lacking anything."*

Psalm 55:22, *"Cast your cares on the Lord and He will sustain you; He will never let the righteous fall."*

Psalm 138:3, *"On the day I called, you answered me; my strength of soul you increased" (ESV).*

📷 **STEP THREE:** *Expect that as Christ-followers* ~ we will have trouble.

📷 **John 16:33,** *"I have told you these things so that in me you will have peace. In this world you will have trouble. But take heart! I have overcome the world."*

📷 **Psalm 22:11,** *"Do not be far from me, because trouble is near and there is no one to help."*

📷 **Psalm 9:9,** *"The Lord is a refuge for the oppressed a stronghold in times of trouble."*

📷 **STEP FOUR:** *Embrace the belief that because God is in control* ~ things will out according to His plan.

📷 **Nahum 1:7,** *"The Lord is good, a refuge in times of trouble. He cares for those who trust in Him."*

📷 **Romans 8:28,** *"And we know that in all things God works for the good of those who love Him, who have been called according to His purpose."*

📷 **Isaiah 55:8,** *"'For my thoughts are not your thoughts, neither are my ways your ways, 'declares the Lord."*

Trouble is something we will never escape until we leave this world. When we accept that we will experience trials, and then embrace that God is with us, it doesn't feel as overwhelming. If we rely on God completely, our faith will strengthen and our character will mature.

📷 **Steps Recapped:**

1. *Believe that no matter what the circumstances* ~ God is with you.

2. *Take control over your emotions* ~ remain calm and faithful.

3. *Expect that as Christ-followers* ~ we will have trouble.

4. *Embrace the belief that because God is in control* ~ things will work out according to His plan.

📷 **Zoom In:** Joseph is a shepherd taking care of his flock with his family. His brothers become jealous and sell him to Ishmaelites traveling to Egypt. He is then sold to one of Pharaoh's leaders, Potiphar, and goes to live with him and runs his household. God blesses Joseph with favor, and that favor pours out onto Potiphar. Potiphar's wife tries to seduce Joseph, but because of Joseph's character and faithfulness to God, as well as Potiphar, Joseph flees the situation. Potiphar's wife lies and says Joseph tried to attack her. Potiphar throws Joseph into prison.

📷 **Life Lesson Learned:** Joseph's story shows us that there will be times when bad things happen to good people. There will be times when we will be mistreated or misconstrued, and truths will be stretched and our integrity challenged. God never wastes moments in our lives. He is building into our character, strengthening our gifts, and maturing us in our faith. The difficult trials are the times to embrace God, allow Him to be our defender, and believe in Him for a fabulous outcome. He's in the plan. He's in the process. He's in your future.

📷 Questions:

1. Why do you think Joseph had so much favor with God? Do you have the favor of the Lord in your life?

2. Scripture indicates that Joseph was thrown in a pit and into prison without fighting back. Do you think it would have made any difference if Joseph stood up for himself?

3. Give an example of a time when someone stretched the truth about you and created havoc in your life? What were your reactions/actions when the truth was obscured or lost?

4. Have you ever experienced a time when you faced many problems at once? How did you respond to those troubles? How did you respond to God?

Look Up:

1. Psalm 28:6

2. Psalm 59:16

3. Psalm 147:11

4. Isaiah 41:13

Songs:

Hymn: "It Is Well With My Soul" *(Horatio Spafford)*

Contemporary: "Blessed Be Your Name" *(Matt Redman)*

Closing Prayer:

Dear Jesus,
Whenever I face adversity,
it is my tendency
to run and hide.

I don't want problems and yet
I know that you can use trouble
to teach me valuable life lessons.

Through these trials,
You can build attributes
into my character that are necessary
to become more like You.

Help me seek You
in the trials, and to learn
and grow through them.

In Jesus' Name, Amen.

CHAPTER 3
Betrayal 📷

When everything seems to be going against you, remember that the
airplane takes off against the wind, not with it.

Henry Ford

📷 **Snapshot:** Last week we learned that every one of us will deal
with trials and troubles. When we trust in God, we will learn through
our struggles and be able to become stronger in our faith.

"Wait a minute, Dale," I said. "I need you to slow down, start at the
beginning, and don't spare any details!"

I felt protective as my friend began to tell me the saga that he was
trudging through at his work. It had been five years since I had first sat
across the table from him. He had served as a co-worship director at a
large church for seven years, and lived for God and loved leading others
in worshiping Him.

Dale continually portrayed a gentle spirit. He leaned toward
incorporating anything that sounded faintly remote to the seventies,
and loved everything that encompassed serving his church, worship
team, and staff.

At our monthly worship director meetings, Dale always added humor,
encouragement, and expertise, because he was just a tad bit older than
the rest of us, by about twenty years. We never left those meetings
without feeling Dale understood us and stood up for us in our own
personal corners.

Now as I listened on the other end of my phone, I could not believe what he was saying. "It started about six months ago. Remember the young guy who has been coming with me and Patricia (the other co-worship director) to the meetings?" he asked.

"Sure, Tad, the young kid who looks like he's twelve," I replied.

"That's him!" he said. "Well, come to find out there was some intricate plan all along to cast me out and bring him in," he finished with a catch in his voice.

"I don't get it, " I answered.

"Kathy, I'm feeling old. Patricia went out and found this young twenty-something guitar player and is working solely with him. She called me into my own office and said that my job was being eliminated. But it wasn't really! No, it was just given to somebody thirty-five years younger. This just can't be happening. I feel so betrayed. Betrayed by my church staff, betrayed by my pastors, and mostly betrayed by my own partner in worship ... the other director. I am in shock. I am sick. What do I do?"

I knew how Dale felt. I had just uncovered the whole escapade of my own marriage and the secret life of my spouse. I knew that feeling of betrayal like the back of my hand. I prayed a silent prayer and began to convey to Dale the same kind of comfort he had given worship directors so many times before.

"Dale, I can't imagine why they thought this was a good plan, and I don't understand how Patricia thinks she can get rid of you without the congregation being angry. You've been their worship director for sixteen years!" I exclaimed.

"But I'm too old now. Apparently, I'm not wanted." he replied in a discouraged tone.

"Look, Dale, Jesus is in this with you. If anyone can understand about betrayal, it is Jesus Christ. I have a bad feeling, Dale, and not only that, I think Patricia and the church are going to be in for a bit of trouble. Whenever Christ's followers are betrayed unjustly, I believe He's going to take care of that in His own time and in His own way. I wouldn't want to be the people involved in this situation," I responded with confidence.

"What will I do?" he asked me.

"God will show you. You need to stay calm, and stay honest. Don't fight; let God defend you. Trust God that somehow He'll reveal something much better for you," I ended a prayer and listened to my friend sob into the phone.

Three months later Dale called me. He sounded happier than he had been in years. A local pastor heard about what happened with Dale and the younger Tad, and offered Dale an amazing job as the sole worship director in a nearby church. Dale received great accolades for his years of experience, knowledge and wisdom, great sense of humor, and on top of that, the congregation embraced him wholeheartedly.

As for Patricia and her young guitarist, well, God's way is so much better than any of our ways. The church board let Patricia go because they hired yet another twenty-something man to go with the young guitarist, Tad. They felt she was too old for the position.

When we are betrayed, we are thrown into a state of shock, hurt, and disbelief. We can't believe that someone would turn on us and we are cut to the core. Jesus knows exactly what it is like to experience betrayal because He dealt with it in His most crucial hours. His disciples fell asleep as He prepared for the cross and prayed in the Garden of Gethsemane (Matthew 26:40-45). One disciple, Judas Iscariot, betrayed him with a kiss and thirty pieces of silver (Matthew 47-50). Being betrayed by others is an overwhelming feeling. Being betrayed by those you trust most is devastating. Webster's dictionary says that the word *betrayed* means "*to deliver somebody or something to an enemy.*"

> Jesus knows exactly what it is like to experience betrayal because He dealt with it in His most crucial hours
>
>

In the story of Joseph, he had been set up for betrayal by his own brothers and by his master's wife.

• **Betrayal 1:** At age seventeen his brothers threw him in the pit and then sold him into slavery.

• **Betrayal 2:** Eleven years later Potiphar's wife lied and turned him over to her husband where he was cast into prison.

• **Betrayal 3:** Joseph's next betrayal came from Pharaoh's cupbearer.

The Hebrew word for cupbearer is *mashqeh*, meaning "*one who gives drink to.*" A cupbearer was an officer of high rank and importance in royal courts. Often chosen for his personal attractiveness, and holding the sole position to protect the king from plots of poison, the cupbearer would possess great influence. He was the chief officer of the household who tasted the wine and passed it to those at the royal table.

At the start of Genesis chapter 40, we see Pharaoh's cupbearer as well as his baker entering the picture.

Look Up: Genesis 40:1-4

"Some time later, the cupbearer and the baker of the king of Egypt offended their master, the king of Egypt. Pharaoh was angry with his two officials, the chief cupbearer and the chief baker, and put them in custody in the house of the captain of the guard, in the same prison where Joseph was confined. The captain of the guard assigned them to Joseph, and he attended them."

The cupbearer and baker must have been in big trouble to have Pharaoh throw them in prison. Fortunately for them, God had been building Joseph's character and producing a great leader in the prison where they will be staying! They will have a leader who is gentle, kind, and wise.

Note that Joseph has not taken a down-and-out attitude. He does not display a defeated mentality. After being thrown into a pit, and now thrown into prison, it seems only natural that he could be downcast, depressed, and even downright mean. Sure, he has taken a turn for the worse, going from pit to prison, but God is with him and because He is with him, everything Joseph works with flourishes.

Joseph didn't allow a bad attitude to take control. He is never once quoted with anger towards God or resentment towards his brothers, Potiphar or Potiphar's wife. Instead, he works hard and waits on God. I often wonder if he thought his story would ever take place inside the confines of Egypt's prison walls, and if he wondered if his future looked impossible.

One of my favorite authors, Beth Moore, states, *"God has a will for your life, Christ has a Word for your life, and the Holy Spirit has a way for your life. Nothing is impossible."*

God is doing what only God can do in Joseph's life. He's taking the bad that happens and making it into something really, really great!

Remember, God has given Joseph the ability to have prophetic dreams. Now, God will give Joseph a new ability, one where he discerns dreams.

Look Up: Genesis 40:5-8

"Each of the two men, the cupbearer and the baker of the King of Egypt, who were being held in prison had a dream the same night, and each dream had a meaning of its own. When Joseph came to them the next morning, he saw that they were dejected. So he asked Pharaoh's officials who were in custody with him in his master's house, 'Why are your faces so sad today?' 'We both had dreams,' they answered, 'but there is no one to interpret them.' Then Joseph said to them, 'Do not interpretations belong to God? Tell me your dreams.'"

Notice that Joseph gives God the credit here. He doesn't tell them, "I am so incredibly special and I have this wonderful gift to be able to interpret dreams." No, instead he acknowledges that his special gift came from the Almighty Creator. What a wonderful reminder to us that when we give God the glory, He honors us by using us.

Last week we discussed why Joseph had "the favor of God." We discovered that God's favor was on Joseph because he was:

1) **faithful**

2) **it was part of God's plan and now we see**

3) **Joseph gives God the glory and doesn't take the credit.**

Modern day experts report that most people dream four to six times a night, that dreams may last from five minutes to thirty minutes or longer and, most often, people don't even remember dreaming.

Yet, two Old Testament men, the cupbearer and the baker, not only remember their dreams, but scripture says they were "dejected."

The cupbearer tells Joseph his dream where he sees a vine in front of him that has three branches. As soon as the vine is budded and blossoms, the clusters ripen into grapes. He sees himself holding Pharaoh's cup, squeezes the grapes into the cup and gives it to Pharaoh. The cupbearer has no idea what it means.

Joseph interprets the dream for him.

Look Up: Genesis 40:12-15

"'This is what it means,' Joseph said to him. 'The three branches are three days. Within three days Pharaoh will lift up your head and restore you to your position, and you will put Pharaoh's cup in his hand, just as you used to do when you were his cupbearer. But when all goes well with you, remember me and show me kindness; mention me to Pharaoh and get me out of this prison. For I was forcibly carried off from the land of the Hebrews, and even here I have done nothing to deserve being put in a dungeon.'"

For a moment, we can feel sad with Joseph. Although he doesn't complain, he does speak the truth to the cupbearer when he says he was taken from his home (notice how he goes all the way back to where the first betrayal happened at his home in Canaan where he was unjustly imprisoned).

God allowed the betrayal and imprisonment of Godly men for a purpose. God doesn't create evil and sin, but at times He allows it for a bigger purpose. It is the plan. It is in the storyline and it ends up being for the best. Always!

Next, Joseph will listen to the baker's dream. Unfortunately for the baker, things don't go as well for him as they did for the cupbearer.

The baker tells Joseph that he had a dream where he had three baskets of bread on his head. In the top basket were baked goods for Pharaoh but the birds were eating them out of the basket right off the top of his head.

I am sure that Joseph must have been a bit squeamish giving the baker the interpretation of his dream.

Look Up: Genesis 40:18-19

"'This is what it means,' Joseph said. 'The three baskets are three days. Within three days Pharaoh will lift off your head and hang you on a tree. And the birds will eat away your flesh.'"

Scripture doesn't give us any details as to what their crimes were, other than they "offended their master." Perhaps through Joseph's interpretation, God wanted the cupbearer and the baker to repent and turn back to God.

Look Up: Genesis 40:20-22

"Now the third day was Pharaoh's birthday, and he gave a feast for all his officials. He lifted up the heads of the chief cupbearer and the chief baker in the presence of his officials. He restored the chief cupbearer to his position, so that he once again put the cup into Pharaoh's hand, but he hanged the chief baker, just as Joseph had said to them in his interpretation."

We see through the interpretations that God showed Joseph (and the others) that God truly spoke through the dreams and used Joseph to deliver the future. Perhaps Joseph held the truths of his interpretations tightly within the walls of his heart and mind, so he could believe in the dreams God gave to him concerning his own family, and how one day they would come true. For just as Joseph held onto his faith, he also embraced hope.

Why would God give the cupbearer and baker dreams? Why were they so disturbed by them and needed someone to interpret them? It was all part of God's plan to use Joseph as an interpreter so that as we move through the story, he will be respected and remembered as someone who God speaks through to interpret. It is as though the negative is being developed and we're beginning to see a bigger picture!

Joseph sees the cupbearer leave and clings to the hope that he has helped him and now the cupbearer will return that kindness. But it doesn't happen that way.

Look Up: Genesis 40:23

"The chief cupbearer, however, did not remember Joseph; he forgot him."

Joseph has done his best in serving those in the prison. He has been a good leader, a Godly leader, a caring leader, and in spite of all that good leadership, he has once again been betrayed. Not on purpose this time, like his brothers and Potiphar's wife's betrayal, but by someone who he treated well and trusted, hoping that his goodness would be reciprocated. Except it was not; it was forgotten.

Betrayal comes in different forms. It can come from your sister taking a treasured possession from the family home that was promised to you. It can come from your neighbor as they call the city to complain about your beloved barking dog. It can come from a co-worker who is stealing your ideas and trying to step over you to get a promotion.

Betrayal can come in the form of a cheating spouse, a child turning on you, a church asking you to worship elsewhere, someone disclosing a secret that you have carried, or even your closest friend walking away when you let them know about your cancer because they don't know how to deal with it. Betrayal always involves loss ... the loss of trust ... the loss of a relationship ... the loss of confidence.

Sometimes we can pinpoint the whys of betrayal and connect it with a severe case of jealousy (such as Joseph's brothers) or we can connect it with revenge (like Potiphar's wife).

At other times, we may not understand why people betray us. Some people may forget about us. Some people may leave us. Some people may ignore us. Others may walk away from us in our greatest times of need. But the comforting news is that God will never leave us. His plans, His ways, and His desires are all meant for our best.

Within your own story, are you in a place right now where someone has betrayed you? Maybe it was your spouse, your elderly parent, your co-worker, or your dearest friend. You feel that pain so deeply. The disappointment is giving your story a negative twist.

It's time to develop a new life story. There are great things in store for Joseph and God's plan is for Joseph's best, even when others disappoint him. That's the same plan God has for your story, because He's always looking out for your best interests. God's got your back ... and your front ... and your shoulders ... and your heart.

Here are some steps that will help when you find yourself dealing with betrayal.

STEP ONE: *Step back and gain perspective* ~ while you get your thoughts and emotions under control.

📷 **II Peter 1:5-9,** *"For this very reason, make every effort to add to your faith goodness; and to goodness, knowledge; and to knowledge, self-control; and to self-control, perseverance; and to perseverance, godliness; and to godliness brotherly kindness; and to brotherly kindness, love. For if you possess these qualities in increasing measure, they will keep you from being ineffective and unproductive in your knowledge of our Lord Jesus Christ."*

📷 **Proverbs 16:32,** *"Better a patient man than a warrior, a man who controls his temper than one who takes a city."*

📷 **Proverbs 18:15,** *"The heart of the discerning acquires knowledge; the ears of the wise seek it out."*

📷 STEP TWO: *Check your heart, attitudes, and motives* ~ to stay upright and Godly.

📷 **Galatians 5:17,** *"For the sinful nature desires what is contrary to the Spirit, and the Spirit what is contrary to the sinful nature. They are in conflict with each other, so that you do not do what you want."*

📷 **Colossians 3:15,** *"Let the peace of Christ rule in your hearts, since as members of one body you were called to peace. And be thankful."*

📷 **John 13:34-35,** *"A new command I give you: Love one another. As I have loved you, so you must love one another. By this all men will know that you are my disciples, if you love one another."*

📷 **STEP THREE:** *Don't try to repay others with sinful actions ~* and hurt the person who betrayed you.

> 📷 **Romans 12:17,** *"Do not repay anyone evil for evil."*

> 📷 **Romans 12:19,** *"Do not take revenge, my friends, but leave room for God's wrath, for it is written: 'It is mine to avenge. I will repay,' says the Lord."*

> 📷 **Luke 6:37,** *"Do not judge, and you will not be judged. Do not condemn, and you will not be condemned. Forgive, and you will be forgiven."*

📷 **STEP FOUR:** *Forgive, forget, and learn ~* from the situation.

> 📷 **Matthew 6:14-15,** *"For if you forgive other people when they sin against you, your heavenly Father will also forgive you. But if you do not forgive others their sins, your Father will not forgive your sins."*

> 📷 **Ephesians 4:32,** *"Be kind and compassionate to one another, forgiving each other, just as in Christ God forgave you."*

> 📷 **Colossians 3:13,** *"Bear with each other and forgive whatever grievances you may have against one another. Forgive as the Lord forgave you."*

📷 **Steps Recapped:**

1. Step back and gain perspective ~ while you get your thoughts and emotions under control.

2. Check your heart, attitudes, and motives ~ to stay upright and Godly.

3. Don't try to repay others with sinful actions ~ and hurt the person who betrayed you.

4. Forgive, forget, and learn ~ from the situation.

Betrayal is a picture of our life that gets totally out of focus. We try to adjust the camera lens and rip the unpleasant pages from our life's story. We allow betrayal to reside in our heart. It is easy to be offended and bitter, but the wise choice is to give it over to God and let Him handle it.

Zoom In: Joseph lived with Potiphar for years and was a Godly leader, taking care of everything in Potiphar's possession. When he couldn't be seduced by Potiphar's wife, she lied and betrayed him before Potiphar. Angered, Potiphar threw Joseph in prison, but even in prison, God's favor rested on Joseph. Pharaoh's cupbearer and baker offended Pharaoh and were thrown into prison with Joseph. After they experienced troubling dreams, God used Joseph to decipher the dreams. Once they came true and the cupbearer was released, Joseph asked him to remember him before Pharaoh, but the cupbearer forgot him. Betrayal is difficult for us to go through, but we read that Joseph remained faithful and positive, rejecting any thoughts of anger or bitterness.

Life Lesson Learned: God wants us to love and forgive those who have hurt and betrayed us. This will never be easy, but with God's help, we can do it. If we don't, that hurt that has entered our heart will take up residency and get the better of us. It will take over and begin to morph and shape our spirit. The betrayer has not only wounded us, but their sin will continue to hurt us unless we forgive them and only then will we be released from the wound.

Questions:

1. Even though Joseph was a prisoner, he maintained a Godly attitude and was kind and helpful to the cupbearer and the baker. In what ways do you struggle with keeping a good attitude towards others when things are not going your way?

2. Recall Joseph being betrayed and then think of a time when you experienced betrayal or were disappointed in someone. What are the similarities between Joseph and your experience?

3. What comes to mind in response to the questions: "What has hurt you? Who has lied about you? Who has betrayed you?" How does God want you respond to someone after they have hurt you?

Λ

xᴼ

4. Are you holding a grudge or harboring bad feelings towards someone who has hurt you? What should you do after reading today's lesson?

📷 **Look Up:**

1. John 8:7

2. Luke 17:3-4

3. Romans 12:20

4. Matthew 5:44

📷 **Songs:**

Hymn: "What a Friend We Have In Jesus" *(Joseph M. Scriven)*
Contemporary: "That's Why We Praise Him" *(Tommy Walker)*

Closing Prayer:

Dear Jesus,
So many times people let me down,
disappoint me, discourage me,
and I become hurt and wounded.

Sometimes that hurt is set
so deep into my soul
that it is hard to imagine
I could ever forgive and forget.

Please, Lord, help me to be like You.
Help me to call on You
and depend on Your help.

Give me the capability to
forgive those who have sinned against
me, and please dear Lord, forgive me for
those who I have hurt and offended.

In Jesus' Name, Amen.

Chapter 4

Faith 📷

The world tells you "You need to see it to believe it."
But God says just the opposite.
Only as you believe it will you ever see it.

Joel Osteen

📷 **Snapshot:** Last week we learned that betrayal is a difficult thing to navigate through, but when we are relying on God, He expects us to let go of our hurts, forgive those who have wounded us, and move ahead with the faith that He is not only the Great Defender, but He is our comforter and our only hope.

The winter wind was whipping icy pellets against our sliding glass door. I peered out to see if the school bus was on time for our regular morning pick up.

Alexis, nine years old on the day I am remembering, said very matter of factly, "Mom, today is show-and-tell for all of the kids with names starting with the letter 'A' in our class. I really want to show them my new ring. Please, Mom, please!"

"Lexi," I answered, "it's fourteen karat gold and we can't risk losing it. Even though it isn't very expensive, it's a snowy winter's day and you'll be wearing mittens. No, honey, the answer is no."

"But, Mom!! All the girls have been show-and-telling their jewelry. Nobody in my class has a ring," she whined.

I knew better. The judgment call had been made and the "no" I gave to Lexi should have remained firm, but she looked so desperate, and I was so cold and tired as I stood in the front entry way still wearing my flannel pajamas.

My daughters had lined up in the front hall in their boots and heavy winter coats, while wooly mittens were thrust upon their hands and scarves were tied tightly around their necks. I was already beginning to worry about how much snow we would get by the end of the school day.

Alexis waited until the very last minute when she could hear the bus coming down the road and made one last attempt to sway me, "Please, Mommy."

I gave in and she ran back to the counter, took off her mittens, and put the pretty little gold ring on her finger. I could see how proud she was of the newly acquired birthday gift.

"Whatever you do, don't lose it," I said as I kissed the girls and sent them down the driveway to meet the bus.

As the morning wore on, the sun burst through the clouds and it was a lovely winter's day. I busied myself with laundry, dishes, and tidying up the house.

After lunch it happened! The phone rang and I got that wonderful mother radar that we get so often. I knew it would be my child. I was certain I would hear about a lost ring as I picked up the phone and answered, "Hello?"

Crying ensued and loud sobs across the phone were heard as I said, "Honey, you're okay, it's okay, take a deep breath and tell me what happened."

"I lost it! Me and Lizbeth were out playing at recess. My hands were so cold, but Mommy I didn't take my mittens off. I already did show-and-tell and everyone loved my ring. Mrs. Haberstash loved it and said it was bea-u-ti-ful." My child could barely get the words out.

"I'll be there at 3:30 to pick you up, honey. Try not to worry about it. I'll pray about it and you pray about it, okay?" I asked her.

"Okay, Mom. I'll pray," she said and hung up the phone.

I went to my knees and hit the floor in prayer. "Please, dear Lord, I cried, please help my baby to believe in You and the power of prayer. She is going to pray, just like she prays every day about things, and she's just a little girl. She has no idea where it is and she's going to have faith in You that she will find a tiny little gold ring in the middle of a winter's day, at school, on the playground, underneath a ton of snow. This is the impossible and this is my prayer ... please help my baby find her ring."

The 3:30 pick-up time could not come fast enough. I parked my car at the school and headed inside to get Alexis. The neighbor was meeting the other girls at the bus so they were covered and we could be there for as long as it took to find a tiny fourteen karat gold ring amidst the winter's snow.

Lexi showed me where she played and I thought to myself, this will be impossible. Track marks of children's snow boots covered the playground. I knew that at least 355 children had been by that same swingset and trampled in that same snow.

It was at that moment of doubt that I heard her small little voice praying. I can still cry when I think of that prayer. "Dear, God, this is my new ring. It's so pretty. Please, God, please help me find it. I'm so sorry I didn't listen to Mommy. Please, God, I know You can do it. Find it for me," my nine year old prayed.

"Mommy," Alexis said, "God will find it. I know He will!"

My hope was renewed by the little voice with child-like faith. We cupped our hands and gently dug through the mounds of snow. After about twenty minutes, I removed my gloves and kept digging until my hands were red and frozen. Then I heard the exclamation, "Mom! It's here. It's by the slide! God found it. He found it!"

Notice that God did not allow me to find the ring, but Alexis found it and it brought joy to my little child's heart as she gave God the credit exclaiming what He had done!

I began to cry. In the mounds of snow that had been compressed by the children's boots, on that winter afternoon, God showed us a tiny gold ring amidst the impossible. My child's faith was honored and matured, while my faith was strengthened and renewed.

The journey of faith can be a challenging one. It can stretch and pull us until we feel we have no more elasticity. On days when we really need it, at times it cannot be found, and at other times, we see the hand of God so clearly and are reminded of His faithfulness through simple things ... even the prayers of a child.

> The journey of faith can be a challenging one. It can stretch and pull us until we feel we have no more elasticity.

The Hebrew word for faith is *emunah*. The Ancient Hebrew Research Center says this about the word emunah, *"The Hebrew root aman means firm, something that is supported or secure. This word is used in Isaiah 22:23 for a nail that is fastened to a 'secure' place. Derived from this root is the word emun meaning a craftsman. A craftsman is one who is firm and secure in his talent. Also derived from aman is the word emunah meaning firmness,*

something or someone that is firm in their actions. When the Hebrew word emunah is translated as faith, misconceptions of its meaning occur. Faith is usually perceived as a knowing while the Hebrew emunah is a firm action. To have faith in God is not knowing that God exists or knowing that he will act, rather it is that the one with emunah will act with firmness toward God's will."

Having faith and believing in God is not just being still in your faith, knowing that God will help. No, it means that we take firm action in that faith, acting as though God has already done what we need Him to do.

In Genesis chapter 40, we left Joseph inside the walls of prison and walking the prison floors. It would be an easy task for Joseph to give up hope after his brothers have sold him into slavery at age 17, after he had been betrayed by his master's wife and spent 11 years in prison, and after he had been forgotten for 2 years by the one person (Pharaoh's cupbearer) who might have been able to get him released, it would be an easy task to give up hope. However, this entire time, God had been developing strong character traits within the soul of this young thirty-year-old and Joseph did not give up remaining hopeful or faithful.

The preacher, Charles Spurgeon, says, *"Don't you know that day dawns after night, showers displace drought, and spring and summer follow winter? Then, have hope! Hope forever for God will not fail you!"*

At the beginning of chapter 41, we read that now Pharaoh is having troubling dreams, but no one not the magicians of Egypt or all its wise men, could interpret them. It's an "aha" moment for the cupbearer when we read that his memory bank is suddenly jolted as he remembers Joseph interpreting his own dream.

Look Up: Genesis 41:9

"Then the chief cupbearer said to Pharaoh, 'Today I am reminded of my shortcomings. Pharaoh was once angry with his servants, and he imprisoned me and the chief baker in the house of the captain of the guard. Each of us had a dream the same night, and each dream had a meaning of its own. Now a young Hebrew was there with us, a servant of the captain of the guard. We told him our dreams, and he interpreted them for us, giving each man the interpretation of his dream. And things turned out exactly as he interpreted them to us. I was restored to my position, and the other man was hanged.' So Pharaoh sent for Joseph ..."

Joseph is told that Pharaoh wants to see him. He shaves, changes clothes, and heads to *the palace*. Perhaps he is excited, perhaps he is fearful, but whatever the emotions, he knows that God has been with him and God will not leave him. He walks the sand from *prison floors* to *palace floors* and enters to face his Egyptian leader.

Look Up: Genesis 41:15

"Pharaoh said to Joseph, 'I had a dream, and no one can interpret it. But I have heard it said of you that when you hear a dream you can interpret it.'"

Once again, he is called upon to interpret the dreams of others, and once again Joseph gives all the glory and the credit to God for his ability.

Look Up: Genesis 41:16

"'I cannot do it,' Joseph replied to Pharaoh, 'but God will give Pharaoh the answer he desires.'"

Not only does Joseph give God the credit, but there is no doubt in Joseph's mind that God will give Pharaoh the answer! Once again God is going to speak through Joseph's willing, obedient, and faithful heart, to help His purpose become real and tangible. He has a plan and these two men are part of a bigger picture.

So often we wonder why bad things are happening to good people. We ask God why He allows troubles, trials, persecution, beatings and death. We gripe and complain. We think that God has turned his head from us and others in their time of need, but we learn from Joseph that God is always with us, even through all of the bad.

I believe it all comes back to the same thing ... God uses the bad people to push us forward to get us to where He needs us to be.

Author of the book *From Dream to Destiny*, Robert Morris, says, *"The Hebrew word for* 'prospering' *means* 'to push forward,' *or* 'make progress;' *and the Greek word for* 'prospering' *means* 'to help on the road.' *In other words, if you* 'prosper' *other people, you help them along the road. If you* 'prosper' *others, you push them forward; you help them get farther along than they were."*

What a contradiction for our thoughts isn't it! That those people who offend us, lie about us, create trouble for us, are the same people who can actually be used by God to help push us to the next place! Think about it for a moment, God uses others to push us along to the next place, the next job, the next thing for your life story.

Within the Bible story, God used Joseph's brothers to get him in *the pit* and to Potiphar and there he becomes a leader. Next, God used Potiphar's wife to get him to *the prison*, and he continues to develop his faith and leadership skills. Now we see God using the cupbearer's forgetfulness to get him to Pharaoh and *the palace*.

If Joseph had not been from the *pit floor* to the *prison floor*, would he be at the *palace floor*? Would Joseph ever have deepened his faith in God? Would Joseph ever have discovered that he held leadership abilities deep within his being?   Would Joseph ever have deepened his character by resisting temptation? Would Joseph's faith ever have been tried in such difficult situations if he was still his daddy's boy back home wearing his lovely coat? The bad people with the bad troubles have pushed him to a higher level. They have helped him to become a better person. Did the over-powering, ever-coddling love of Jacob help him mature into who God needed him to be? No! The bad people did and faith in God was stretched, nurtured, and matured.

In my own personal life, I know that God has used my hardest and most difficult times to grow me the most and push me the farthest on this journey between beginning and end. I never want to stop remembering what God has done in me, through me, and for me. Like Joseph, the biggest challenges have come to me through trials, and the greatest opportunities to grow in my faith have been in those same opportunities.

🔲 **Look Up: Genesis 41:17-21**

"Then Pharaoh said to Joseph, 'In my dream I was standing on the bank of the Nile, when out of the river there came up seven cows, fat and sleek, and they grazed among the reeds. After them, seven other cows came up-scrawny and very ugly and lean. I had never seen such ugly cows in all the land of Egypt. The lean, ugly cows ate up the seven fat cows that came up first. But even after they ate them, no one could tell that they had done so; they looked just as ugly as before. Then I woke up.'"

This is Pharaoh's first dream.

Throughout scripture, God uses certain numbers repeatedly. In last week's lesson, we saw that God used the number *three* within the cupbearer's dream (Genesis 40:12), as well as the baker's dream (Genesis 40:18). Three is used throughout scripture in many stories such as Jonah in the belly of the fish for three days and three nights, Esther asks the Jews to pray for three days and three nights, and Jesus was crucified, buried, and raised from the dead on the third day.

God also uses the number seven frequently in scripture as a number of completeness and perfection. He created the world and everything in it over a seven day period, there were seven "I AM" statements in the Gospel of John that Jesus used when He spoke of Himself. Jesus also mentions seven parables in Matthew 13, and Joshua marched around the city of Jericho seven times. In this passage in Genesis 41, Pharaoh's dream involves the number seven.

📷 Look Up: Genesis 41:22-24a

"In my dreams I also saw seven heads of grain full and good, growing on a single stalk. After them, seven other heads sprouted-withered and thin and scorched by the east wind. The thin heads of grain swallowed up the seven good heads ..."

Now we will see the picture as it begins to come into focus. While on a vacation, my husband Dean and I purchased a camera on clearance. It offered so many great features, one was the ability to take close ups. For the first time ever, the picture was in clear focus and we were able to value, appreciate, and understand things at a closer level than before. That is what is happening in Joseph's life. God will reveal to us why Joseph has suffered through these years, why Joseph's faith in God has deepened and not faltered, and we will learn from his life lessons.

God is faithful to Joseph and reveals the dreams to Pharaoh through Joseph's interpretations.

Look Up: Genesis 41:25-27

"Then Joseph said to Pharaoh, 'the dreams of Pharaoh are one and the same. God has revealed to Pharaoh what He is about to do. The seven good cows are seven years, and the seven good heads of grain are seven years; it is one and the same dream. The seven lean, ugly cows that came up afterward are seen years, and so are the seven worthless heads of grain scorched by the east wind; they are seven years of famine.'"

Then Joseph tells Pharaoh that God has shown him what He is about to do. For seven years Egypt will have an abundance of food throughout the land, but seven years of severe famine will follow.

God always has a purpose in the process. There is never any happenstance with Him and what He's allowing, or doing in our lives. Joseph lets Pharaoh know that God's plan is twofold:

1) It has been decided by God that this will happen.

2) God will do this soon.

Because Pharaoh has this dream two times, you can see the determination of God to not only make it clear, but to make it emphatic.

God will use the willing, the obedient, and the faithful to further His purposes. No one stands in God's way. Scripture tells us in Revelation 3:7 *"These are the words of Him who is holy and true, who holds the key of David. What He opens no one can shut, and what He shuts no one can open."* God alone is in control. Why is our faith lacking? Why is our faith shaken?

Utilizing the skills of leadership that are now sharpened, Joseph provides Pharaoh with his next steps. He says:

1) Look for a wise and discerning leader and put him in charge.

2) Appoint commissioners over the land to take a fifth of the harvest of Egypt during the seven years of abundance.

3) Collect the food in the good years and store up grain.

4) Food should be stored in reserve for the country to be used in the famine.

Look Up: Genesis 41:39-40

"Then Pharaoh said to Joseph, 'Since God has made all this known to you, there is no one so discerning and wise as you. You shall be in charge of my palace, and all my people are to submit to your orders. Only with respect to the throne will I be greater than you.'"

Remember the following words that were from Joseph's dream:

Look Up: Genesis 37:5-8

"Joseph had a dream, and when he told it to his brothers, they hated him all the more. He said to them, 'Listen to this dream I had: We were binding sheaves of grain out in the field when suddenly my sheaf rose and stood upright, while your sheaves gathered around mine and bowed down to it.' His brother said to him, 'Do you intend to reign over us? Will you actually rule us?' And they hated him all the more because of his dream and what he had said."

All of the jealousy, adversity, and betrayal did not press him to waiver in his faith, but instead God rewards that steadfastness. Perhaps after remaining in prison those extra two years, Joseph may have just mustered up a tiny bit of faith, but nevertheless, it has still been there in the corners of his heart and God sees it and honors it.

At times we are like Alexis digging through the snow, searching for our treasured possession and mustering up a tiny bit of faith. Faith doesn't come easily to everyone. For some, they have discovered that comfortable place of security where they know and believe that God is in control. For others, it is a day-in day-out struggle to remind themselves that scripture tells us we must be faithful in order to be obedient to God and please Him.

Look Up: Hebrews 11:6

"And without faith, it's impossible to please God because anyone who comes to Him must believe that He exists and that He rewards those who earnestly seek Him."

Even God's greatest Biblical heroes had their own moments of struggling with faith. So often, we saw the disciples questioning Jesus because they didn't understand. Jesus wanted them to just trust Him and quit with all the questions.

Max Lucado, one of my favorite prolific authors writes, *"We need to remember that the disciples were common men given a compelling task. Before they were the stained-glassed saints in the windows of cathedrals, they were somebody's next-door-neighbors trying to make a living and raise a family. They weren't cut from theological cloth or raised on supernatural milk. But they were an ounce more devoted than they were afraid and, as a result, did some extraordinary things."*

Joseph becomes the administrative head of the kingdom, a position sometimes designated as vizier. Joseph was appointed vizier as a reward for his talent and served as a modern day prime minister.

📷 **Look Up: Genesis 4141-42, 43b**

"So Pharaoh said to Joseph, 'I hereby put you in charge of the whole land of Egypt.' Then Pharaoh took his signet ring from his finger and put it on Joseph's finger. He dressed him in robes of fine linen and put a gold chain around his neck ... Thus he put him in charge of the whole land of Egypt."

The use of Pharaoh's seal and his signet ring would indicate that Joseph was Pharaoh's primary representative in administrative matters. Pharaoh has given Joseph great leadership and authority over his entire kingdom, and along with that Pharaoh changed Joseph's name to Zaphenath-Pa-neah. This was to show the Egyptian people that Pharaoh accepted him completely as an Egyptian and as the authority over their land. Joseph's connection to the past would be severed.

Along with the authority and name change came a wife. Pharaoh gave Joseph a wife named, Asenath, the daughter of Potiphera, priest of On. Scripture makes no mention as to any opposition of this marriage, even though Asenath was the daughter of a pagan priest. At age thirty, Joseph is now married and his story has journeyed from the severity of *the pit,* to *the prison,* to *the palace.*

Because of Joseph's faithfulness to God and obedience in honoring the dreams that God gave to Pharaoh, just like Alexis gave credit to God for the found ring, Joseph collected the food and stored it in the cities.

📷 **Look Up: Genesis 41:49**

"Joseph stored up huge quantities of grain, like the sand of the sea: it was so much that he stopped keeping records because it was beyond measure."

Joseph and his wife have two sons. The first he named Manasseh and said, "It is because God has made me forget all my trouble and all my father's household" (Genesis 41:51), and the second son he named Ephraim and said, "It is because God has made me fruitful in the land of my suffering"(Genesis 41:52).

The seven years of abundance in Egypt took place and then seven years of famine began, but because of Joseph's wisdom and leadership, Egypt had plenty of food.

Look Up: Genesis 41:56

"When the famine had spread over the whole country, Joseph opened the storehouses and sold grain to the Egyptians, for the famine was severe throughout Egypt. And all the countries came to Egypt to buy grain from Joseph, because the famine was severe in all the world."

There will be situations in our lives where it will be very difficult to remain faith filled. We will struggle with the how, the why, and the why me? We will be digging in the impossible mounds of icy cold snow, desperately seeking an answer for help from God.

Perhaps we will be unsure that we can even continue, but as the camera lens zooms in on what God is doing, we will see and begin to grasp that He will be there in the winter afternoons and the spring days, in the bright summer mornings and the brisk fall evenings. He will respond to our minute seeds of mustard-sized belief and we will see the supernatural powers of the loving, living God. We will know that He, and only He, will answer our prayers and return that which was lost ... hope. For in the place between hope and evidence, comes the beautiful and meaningful attitude of faith.

Here are some steps that will encourage you to make each day a powerful declaration to God of strong character and never ending faith in Him.

📷 **STEP ONE:** *Zoom in on how you respond to trouble* and determine if you are faith-filled or continually worried.

> 📷 **II Chronicles 16:9a,** *"For the eyes of the Lord range throughout the earth, to strengthen those whose hearts are fully committed to Him."*

> 📷 **Exodus 15:2,** *"The Lord is my strength and my defense; He has become my salvation. He is my God, and I will praise Him, my father's God, and I will exalt Him."*

> 📷 **Psalm 119:23,** *"Though rulers sit together and slander me, your servant will meditate on your decrees."*

📷 **STEP TWO:** *Confess any doubt* that you are harboring in your heart today.

> 📷 **I John 1:9,** *"If we confess our sins, He is faithful and just and will forgive us our sins and purify us from all unrighteousness."*

> 📷 **Hebrews 8:12,** *"For I will forgive their wickedness and will remember their sins no more."*

> 📷 **Psalm 103:12,** *"As far as the east is from the west, so far has He removed our transgressions from us."*

📷 **STEP THREE:** *Pray and ask God to strengthen your faith* in Him and His watch over your life.

> 📷 **Romans 4:3,** *"What does Scripture say? 'Abraham believed God, and it was credited to him as righteousness.'"*

John 5:24, *"Very truly I tell you, whoever hears My word and believes Him who sent me has eternal life and will not be judged but has crossed over from death to life."*

I Thessalonians 5:17, *"Pray continually."*

STEP FOUR: *Resolve to live your life with the words "By faith ..."*

Joshua 1:9, *"Have I not commanded you? Be strong and courageous. Do not be afraid; do not be discouraged, for the Lord your God will be with you wherever you go."*

I Chronicles 16:11, *"Look to the Lord and His strength; seek His face always."*

Psalm 27:1, *"The Lord is my light and my salvation- whom shall I fear? The Lord is the stronghold of my life—of whom shall I be afraid?"*

Faith is the very core essence of Christianity. We believe that God sent His son, Jesus Christ, to die on the cross for our sins, be buried, rise again on the third day, and provide us with salvation if we confess our sins and profess Him as Lord and Savior.

In order to make God happy, we need to simply believe! Believe that He can do anything He wants to, or needs to, in us, with us, and through us. It is when we make ourselves available in obedience to God that we can see the fruit of our faith. Don't let the obstacles, the deep mounds of snow, or the narrow lens of your camera's eye keep you limited. With faith ... all things are possible!

📷 **Steps Recapped:**

1. Zoom in on how you respond to trouble ~ and determine if you are faith-filled or continually worried.

2. Confess any doubt~ that you are harboring in your heart today.

3. Pray and ask God to strengthen your faith ~ in Him and His watch over your life.

4. Resolve to live your life with the words "By faith ..."

📷 **Zoom In:** Once Joseph interprets the cupbearer's dream and the cupbearer is released, Joseph hopes that he will be remembered, but instead, two years go by and he has been forgotten in prison. Joseph never gives up and remains faithful before God. After Pharaoh has strange dreams, the cupbearer remembers Joseph can interpret dreams and recommends him to Pharaoh. Once the dreams are interpreted, Pharaoh puts Joseph in charge of the country and the crops in preparation for the upcoming famine. Joseph gets married and has two sons.

📷 **Life Lesson Learned:** Joseph remained confident in the God of his youth and consequently loved Him, listened for Him, and lived for Him. His faith was honored all along the pathway in his story, because throughout each step, God was with him. God lifted him out of *the pit*, out of *the prison*, and put him on the floor of *the palace*. Faith in God is unstoppable.

Questions:

1. How do you think Joseph felt when he was forgotten by the cupbearer for another two years? If you were in his shoes, how would you have responded?

2. Do you find that during times of trouble you worry or are you calm and resolve to trust God? Give details of a situation where you struggled with trusting God and believing things would work out for God's best.

3. Think back to a time when you saw the goodness of God through an answer to prayer. Explain the situation, the prayer, and God's answer.

4. If you were to encourage someone today to remain faithful to God no matter what comes their way, how would you articulate that encouragement?

Look Up:

1. Matthew 17:20-21

2. Matthew 21:21

3. Mark 10:52

4. II Timothy 1:7

Songs:

Hymn: "The Solid Rock" *(Edward Mote)*
Contemporary: "One Thing Remains" *(Brian Johnson, Christa Black Gifford, and Jeremy Riddle)*

Closing Prayer:

Dear Jesus,
There are times when I know
I need to be faithful,
and I can only rally myself
to have a tiny drop of faith.

Thank you that Your answers
to prayers are not about the amount
of faith I have,
but rather, that I just have faith.

Please continue to work
in my heart
and strengthen, deepen,
and mature my faith in You.

Help me to believe
in Your will for my life,
even in times of doubt and trouble.

In Jesus' Name, Amen.

CHAPTER 5
Forgiveness 📷

One of the great marks of maturity is to accept the fact that everybody comes "as is."

John Ortberg

📷 **Snapshot:** Last week we learned that faith is the basis of a relationship with Jesus Christ, and God is pleased when we have faith in Him. It is when we make ourselves available in obedience to God that was can see the fruit of our faith. Faith in God is unstoppable!

I put my feet up on the lawn chair and sipped my ice tea in the hot summer sunshine. Grandma K and I had just finished an hour of weeding in her beautiful flower garden. "Are you just going to laze the day away?" she asked.

"Uh, huh," I smiled and answered. "I'm going to enjoy looking at the beauty of the garden now."

Grandma had the most beautiful flowers of anyone I knew, but she was constantly out in the garden weeding. There were certain weeds that grew so quickly and would start to crowd all of the beauty of the gorgeous flowers by overtaking them.

This morning, the weeds were pulled, the flowers were lovely, and I was just going to sit and enjoy them for a few minutes until Gram gave me another task.

The screen door screeched and slammed shut and for whatever reason I'll never understand, as I sat there in that warmth and beauty, my mind was thrust back to a time when things were not so beautiful. I began to drift back in time to a place where, when I am fully cognizant, I will not allow myself to travel.

I could see my pastor's angry red face. I could hear his words once again in my mind as he shouted, "Stop this nonsense! You are just fine. I am not accepting your resignation and you will report to this job tomorrow at the same time as always. How ridiculous!"

I cringed as I remembered his anger. The job had been a blessing for me and God had been building into my abilities of creativity, leadership, and musicianship. However, after four years, trouble had ensued and I was being harassed by a congregational member. As a woman, I took it very seriously. As a man, my boss thought it was my imagination and it would soon pass. It did not, and I no longer felt safe. I submitted a carefully-written and prayed-over resignation that afternoon.

The hard part about working for a church is that when you don't have that job, you don't have a church. My family and I began to search for a new church home, but the truth deep down inside the corridors of my heart had slowly seeped out. I didn't trust anyone, and I certainly didn't trust pastors. In my mind, no church would be comforting.

Days turned into weeks, weeks turned into months, when finally my friend called and said, "Come with us! We're visiting the church down the street from your house."

That Sunday morning, I sent my children to their classes downstairs at the church, while I sat in the back pew, positioned right next to the exit. The music was exceptional, the people friendly, and Pastor Frank was dynamic in delivering his sermon. The only problem was me. I cried through the entire service. I could not control it, I could not understand it, I just cried.

When the final prayer was done, I made a bee line for my children and pushed past everyone with my head down (after all that crying!) trying to get to the door to get out. But, as God would have it, I could not push past the smiling Pastor Frank.

He stooped down and talked with each of my girls, and then looked straight into my eyes, and right past them into my heart. "I'm Frank Riley, and you are?" he asked.

"Kathy," I responded nervously.

"Kathy, I'm so glad you're here. Do you want to come in and see me this week?" he asked like we'd been friends for years.

"Um, I'll think about that," I replied. I knew that he was aware that something was terribly wrong. How could you not? If you're speaking and looking out at the congregation and notice someone crying the entire time, you would think I'm either so great they are moved, I'm either so bad they are moved, or God is talking to them and they are moved.

Three days later, after a kind phone message from Pastor Frank, I showed up to his office. "What's happened in your world, Kathy, to create such hurt?" Pastor Frank asked.

I began to tell him about my time with the church and how painful it was. Pastor Frank listened, supported, and somehow in my mind, brought out a big tube of Neosporin to ease the brutal cuts and bruises of my soul.

After I had concluded and he gave his wonderfully wise words of counsel, he said, "You cannot go on this way, Kathy. Resentment and unforgiveness will be like a wild weed that is growing in the garden of your heart. It will choke out all of the beauty God has for you. You have to let it go, forgive these people, and move forward to what God's plan is for your life."

And then he said the words I would not forget, "Unforgiveness will be the stopping point in your life. You will not move past this point until you forgive."

Of course you know what happened ... I cried ... and cried ... and cried. Pastor Frank waited ... and waited ... and waited. Something broke in me that day. A huge pair of garden clippers came out of my mind and cut away all of the weeds that were stifling growth and goodness, new life, and a future. The tears of repentance for being mad, and forgiveness for those who hurt me, watered the garden of my soul until I began to come back to life.

In those first few minutes of our meeting, my life changed forever. Pastor Frank put me on his staff as a creative volunteer that answered directly to him (once again I trusted), and I spent time at that church healing and growing. Forgiveness was the only means of repairing the weeds that were taking over my spirit.

In the story of Joseph, we know that he has been wounded, but in Genesis 41:51-52, we see that Joseph has had two sons. Through these two sons, we see Joseph's inner soul and we begin to grasp his attitude with forgiving his brothers and Potiphar's wife. Because he has gone from *the pit*, to *the prison*, to *the palace*, it's hard for him to begrudge the facts of where his journey has taken him, and hard to remain angry towards those who wronged him. But it is human nature to have anger and resentment. We all deal with it.

One of my favorite authors and pastors, John Ortberg, says, "*When we enter relationships with the illusion that people are normal, we resist the truth that they are not. We enter an endless attempt to fix them, control*

them, or pretend that they are what they're not."

Being angry, wishing that people were different, and wanting to fix them until they are just like us, is not reality.

Remember in the wonderful old Audrey Hepburn movie, "My Fair Lady," where Professor Higgins says, *"Why can't a woman be more like a man ... why can't a woman be like me?"* If we can control how other people act, we can safeguard ourselves from hurt, but life is not like this at all!

> Being angry, wishing that people were different, and wanting to fix them until they are just like us, is not reality.

Joseph has already been looking into the garden of his soul. He sees the value in forgiving the past and moving on because he doesn't want to have his future strangled out by the weeds of unforgiveness.

 **Look Up: Genesis 41:51-52**

"Joseph named his firstborn Manasseh and said, 'It is because God has made me forget all my trouble and all my father's household.' The second son he named Ephraim and said, 'It is because God has made me fruitful in the land of my suffering.'"

Joseph is working through the process of moving past the hurt and pain. He has a wife and two sons and is in charge of Pharaoh's palace. Days are moving into weeks and weeks into years as we now move into chapter 42. The famine is real and Jacob learns that there is grain in Egypt and sends his sons to get food.

 **Look Up: Genesis 42:3**

"Then ten of Joseph's brothers went down to buy grain from Egypt. But

Jacob did not send Benjamin, Joseph's brother, with the others, because he was afraid that harm might come to him. So Israel's sons were among those who went to buy grain, for the famine was in the land of Canaan also."

Joseph has eleven brothers (Genesis 35:23-26). Jacob's first wife, Leah, had five sons. Then, second and beloved wife, Rachel, had two sons, Joseph and Benjamin (she dies during the childbirth of Benjamin). Then there are two sons from Rachel's maidservant Bilhah, and two sons from Leah's maidservant Zilpah. The true full blood brother of Joseph, through Rachel and Jacob, is Benjamin (his name means "son of my right hand"). Jacob doesn't want a repeat of what happened to Joseph, to happen to his youngest son, Benjamin. He is keeping him at home.

For the first time in twenty years (sold at 17, worked for Potiphar for 11, in prison for 2, and 7 years of storing up grain for the famine),the brothers will face their brother, Joseph, the one whom they betrayed. But interestingly enough, they will not recognize him. Remember, Joseph is the governor of Egypt and is dressed in Egyptian attire and speaking in an Egyptian tongue. Joseph's dream has now come to fruition.

Look Up: Genesis 42:6b

"So when Joseph's brothers arrived, they bowed down to him with their faces to the ground."

Joseph recognizes them immediately but pretends to not know them.

Look Up: Genesis 42:8

"Although Joseph recognized his brothers, they did not recognize him."

He treats them harshly and pushes them, perhaps because he does not see his little brother Benjamin, and maybe that is disconcerting to him. Have they harmed him as well?

 Look Up: Genesis 42:9

"Then he remembered his dreams about them and said to them, 'You are spies! You have come to see where our land is unprotected.'"

We may wonder why the once kind and Godly leader we have read about in previous chapters is now harsh and short with his brothers. Matthew Henry's Commentary states this, *"Joseph had an eye to his dreams, which he knew to be divine, in his carriage towards his brethren, and aimed at the accomplishment of them and the bringing of his brethren to repentance for their former sins; and both these points were gained. He showed himself very rigorous and harsh with them. The very manner of his speaking, considering the post he was in, was enough to frighten them; for he spoke roughly to them ... We may be sure it was not from a spirit of revenge, that he might now trample upon those who had formerly trampled upon him; he was not a man of that temper. But, 1. It was to enrich his own dreams, and complete the accomplishment of them. 2. It was to bring them to repentance. 3. It was to get out of them an account of the state of their family, which he longed to know ... God in his providence sometimes seems harsh with those he loves, and speaks roughly to those for whom yet he has great mercy in store."*

In order to keep his identity secret, he continues to pressure them until they tell him about their family.

 Look Up: Genesis 42:13

"Your servants were twelve brothers, the sons of one man, who lives in the land of Canaan. The youngest is now with our father, and one is no more."

Joseph is still moved towards doing God's will and that means the brothers need to get to a place of repentance. We are always responsible for our own actions. We cannot control others and their actions, but at times, God will call upon us to help those people come to a place of where they see what they have done and we help lead them to repent.

In this instance, God uses Joseph to soften the hearts of his brothers, and scares them, informing them one must return to get Benjamin, and then throws them all into prison! Now they get a feel for what Joseph has been through. But please note, God is using his number "3" again, as He so frequently does in scripture (i.e. Jonah in the fish's belly for three days, Esther prays for three days, Saul blinded for three days, Jesus Christ death and resurrection three days), and now another parallel is drawn between Joseph's story and that of Christ. The parallel is that his brothers will be in prison (tomb) for three days.

Look Up: Genesis 42:17-20

"And he put them all in custody for three days. On the third day, Joseph said to them, 'Do this and you will live, for I fear God: If you are honest men, let one of your brothers stay here in prison, while the rest of you go and take grain back for your starving households. But you must bring your youngest brother to me, so that your words may be verified and that you may not die.' This is what they proceeded to do."

Notice how Joseph is letting them know that even though he is an Egyptian, he "fears God." He is trying to give them comfort. And BOOM! ... there it is in verse 21; their hearts have been softened. It is what I like to call "the switch." "The switch" is where God allows the person who has wronged someone to go through the same kind of situation themselves. They have tried to forget, but now they remember. God's purpose is accomplished.

Look Up: Genesis 42:21

"They said to one another, 'Surely we are being punished because of our brother. We saw how distressed he was when he pleaded with us for his life, but we would not listen; that's why this distress has come upon us.'"

Guilt. Beautiful, glorious, conviction. When we are convicted, it can lead to repentance. They begin talking about their guilt and repentance right in front of their brother, Joseph, unaware that he could understand every word they were saying. I love what Matthew Henry's Commentary says about this verse, *"The benefit of afflictions; they often prove the happy and effectual means of awakening conscience."*

Have you ever been in a situation where something horrifically bad allows your conscience to be pricked and you become acutely aware of the way you acted? I know I certainly have. Joseph's heart in the story is now so keenly evident.

Look Up: Genesis 42:24

"He turned away from them and began to weep ..."

Forgiveness has gone to the garden of his heart and has begun to dig away at the weeds, pulling them one by one, tossing them out. To hear the brothers talk about him, to know that they are sad and remorseful, is too much for Joseph.

At times, we will have others harm us through actions and words, and at times we will receive an apology. But more often than not, we will not receive an apology and will not experience what Joseph did that day ... someone being remorseful about how they treated us. I think that is what makes forgiveness more difficult. It seems so healing when people are sorry and remorseful, but pride often keeps people from saying they are sorry. How sad! What a great lesson for us to remember, that healing comes so freely from the beautiful words, "I'm sorry."

After this, Joseph keeps brother Simeon back with him as a hostage to make sure of the others return. He fills their bags with grain and returns the silver the brothers gave him. The brothers believe this is a trap set for them, and they return home to tell Jacob everything that has happened.

Jacob refuses to send his son Benjamin back with the brothers. Who knows why, but he didn't trust them. After all, Jacob doesn't know what really happened to his beloved Joseph.

But Reuben gives the authority to Jacob to put his children to death if they don't return with Benjamin. Time goes by, but once the grain has been eaten Jacob tells them to go back to Egypt for more food, but Judah reminds him they need Benjamin for the exchange.

Look Up: Genesis 43:9

"I myself will guarantee his safety; you can hold me personally responsible for him ... I will bear the blame before you all my life."

Judah is beginning to feel a bit guilty, isn't he?

The brothers head back with Benjamin to present themselves before Joseph. Jacob has sent back the money plus double, along with balm and honey. They work hard to convince Joseph's steward that they didn't really steal back the money, it just appeared in their sacks. He returned Simeon to their side and they prepared to share Joseph's noon meal at his home.

Look Up: Genesis 43:28

"They replied, 'Your servant our father is still alive and well.' And they

bowed low to pay him honor."

God is so gracious in how we read His Word. Look at those words closely *"... and they bowed low to pay him honor."* There are the brothers, once again, bowing down to Joseph. This builds confidence within our own souls that God is a God of His Word, that Joseph's dreams (God's gift) really were from God, and that His plan and purposes will come to fruition, perhaps not in the snap of our fingers, but in His timing.

Joseph questions the brothers about their father and asks if the extra brother is Benjamin. All of the pain of those years, all of the questions about "why me" and all of the troubles are dug up to the surface as the weed is pulled, loosened, and now removed. Once again, he cries.

📷 **Look Up: Genesis 43:29-30**

"As he looked about and saw his brother Benjamin, his own mother's son, he asked, 'Is this your youngest brother, the one you told me about?' And he said, 'God be gracious to you, my son.' Deeply moved at the sight of his brother, Joseph hurried out and looked for a place to weep. He went into his private room and wept there."

A recent study by physicians shows that emotional tears have a different chemical composition than tears caused by irritants, like onions. It also showed that a major stress hormone called prolactin is released from the body via tears. I am sure Joseph was releasing some built up emotions as the weeds were pulled from his heart.

While they ate lunch, Joseph was served separately from his brothers because Hebrews were detestable to Egyptians, and yet look at how God has worked in this storyline! The very leader of the Egyptians is a Hebrew.

Just to show a small bit of inside humor, perhaps to appease some of that hurt inside his soul, Joseph has the brothers seated from the firstborn to the youngest, and they are surprised. Who knew that inside information? A side note is that Joseph served his brother Benjamin five times the amount the other brothers received.

The beloved and brilliant American educator, Presbyterian minister, songwriter, author, and television host, Fred (Mister) Rogers says this about forgiveness: *"Forgiveness is a strange thing. It can sometimes be easier to forgive our enemies than our friends. It can be hardest of all to forgive people we love."*

Joseph's heart is softened, tears are flowing, and he is obedient to God's will and purposes. Joseph understands that it will take time to recover from the wounds that have been bestowed upon him by others, but the end result is freedom. When we don't release anger, bitterness, and grudges, we are still tied to those people and the moment when we were hurt. We do not experience total freedom until we say, "I choose to forgive, I choose to move forward."

Here are some steps that will encourage you to forgive others, forget those hurts, and look forward to God's blessings upon you when you release it all to Him.

STEP ONE: *Search your heart to see if you are harboring anger, bitterness, resentment, or a grudge* against someone.

Psalm 139:23, *"Search me, God, and know my heart; test me and know my anxious thoughts.."*

Psalm 66:10, *"For you, God, tested us; you refined us like silver."*

Deuteronomy 4:29, *"But if from there you seek the Lord*

your God, you will find Him if you seek Him with all your heart and with all your soul."

STEP TWO: *Confess any sin* and pull out the weeds of hurt.

📷 **II Corinthians 7:9-10,** *"You were made sorrowful to the point of repentance; for you were made sorrowful according to the will of God ... For the sorrow that is according to the will of God produces a repentance without regret, leading to salvation."*

📷 **Psalm 32:1,** *"Blessed is the one whose transgression is forgiven, whose sin is covered."*

📷 **Proverbs 28:13,** *"Whoever conceals his transgressions will not prosper, but he who confesses and forsakes them will obtain mercy" (ESV).*

📷 **STEP THREE: *Imagine being in front of that person*** who hurt you and telling them that you forgive them.

📷 **Matthew 6:14-15,** *"For if you forgive other people when they sin against you, your heavenly Father will also forgive you. But if you do not forgive others their sins, your Father will not forgive your sins."*

📷 **John 8:7,** *"... 'If anyone of you is without sin, let him be the first to throw a stone at her.'"*

📷 **Luke 17:3-4,** *"So watch yourselves. If your brother or sister sins, rebuke them, and if they repent, forgive them. Even if they sin against you seven times in a day, and seven times come back* *to you saying, 'I repent,' you must forgive them."*

STEP FOUR: *Work hard at not letting the weeds of bitterness return to your garden* and overtake the beauty that God is creating.

Romans 12:20, *"On the contrary: 'If your enemy is hungry, feed him; if he is thirsty, give him something to drink. In doing this, you will heap burning coals on his head.'"*

Philippians 4:8, *"Finally, brothers and sisters, whatever is true, whatever is noble, whatever is right, whatever is pure, whatever is lovely, whatever is admirable--if anything is excellent or praiseworthy--think about such things."*

I Thessalonians 5:22, *"Reject every kind of evil."*

Forgiveness is crucial in our Christian walk. We gratefully accept God's forgiveness for our sins, and in doing so, we must extend that same grace to others. When we harbor those feelings of hurt and water them with reminiscing thoughts that play over in our minds, we are not cultivating a garden that is beautiful. Instead, we are taking a snapshot of our garden when it is overtaken with weeds, and framing it, and hanging it in the hallways of our hearts. We must free our hearts from the strangling weeds that confine us, and let God produce freedom.

Steps Recapped:

1. Search your heart to see if you are harboring anger, bitterness, resentment, or a grudge against someone.

2. Confess any sin and pull out the weeds of hurt.

3. Imagine being in front of that person who hurt you and telling them that you forgive them.

4. Work hard at not letting the weeds of bitterness return to your garden and overtake the beauty that God is creating.

📷 **Zoom In:** As time goes by, Joseph is accepted by Pharaoh as a leader of the Egyptians, and he is married and has two sons. Joseph's brothers travel to Egypt because of the famine. They fulfill Joseph's original dreams that they will bow before him. Joseph recognizes them, but they don't recognize him. He challenges them and reminds them of their sin against him, creating remorse within their spirits. Joseph sends them back home and asks them to return with their youngest brother. When they return with the youngest, Benjamin, Joseph breaks down and tells them he is their brother, Joseph. Joseph chooses to forgive and embrace his brothers, as his heart is filled with love and mercy towards them.

📷 **Life Lesson Learned:** Joseph was hurt and wounded by his brothers and his master's wife. They treated him unfairly and it changed the entire course of his life. Instead of remaining bitter and angry, he gives credit to God for helping him, and claims that God has removed the sad memories of his past. He is faced with the opportunity to repay evil or forgive. He forgives and is a better person because of that gracious spirit. Because of his attitude, healing begins and life gets better as we see God's ultimate purpose unfold.

Questions:

1. If you were to change places with Joseph, how would you have responded when you saw your brothers in need right before your eyes? Have you ever been so angry with someone that you can't shake the roots of bitterness?

2. Are you quick to become angry with people when they are in the wrong? Do you hold a grudge easily? How do you express anger?

3. Can you think of someone in your life right now who is stopping you from having a garden free of weeds? How long has this been going on in your heart?

4. Have you ever had to go to someone and ask forgiveness? How did you feel when you received it? How did you feel when that someone did not want to forgive you?

📷 **Look Up:**

1. **Isaiah 43:25-26**

2. **Matthew 6:9-15**

3. **Acts 3:19**

4. **Ephesians 1:7**

📷 **Songs:**

Hymn: "There Is a Fountain" *(William Cowper)*
Contemporary: "Your Grace is Enough" *(Matt Maher)*

Closing Prayer:

Dear Jesus,

Sometimes the pain of what others
have done against me is unbearable.

At times, I find it almost impossible to forgive them
and to forget what they have done.

I don't understand what would
make them want to act in that hurtful way.

Yet I know that I can act out anger
and jealousy and hurt others as well.

Please help me to forgive others
and clear the roots of bitterness
out of my heart and soul.

Help me to not cling to offenses
and love others like you do.

In Jesus' Name, Amen.

CHAPTER 6

Reconciliation 📷

We are one people forever woven together in a tapestry,
... and it is our job, our duty and our great challenge to fight the
voices of division and to seek the salve of reconciliation.

Roy Barnes

📷 **Snapshot:** Last week we learned that when we harbor bitterness in our hearts after someone has hurt us, it can be like a weed in a garden that chokes out life and beauty. When Joseph forgave his brothers, healing began in their relationship and God was able to work His purposes through Joseph's life, as well as use Joseph to save those who were starving, including his own family.

The hallway was so quiet that all I could hear was the resounding squeak of my tennis shoes rubbing against the shiny, waxed linoleum floor. I felt kind of nervous and wondered how I get myself into these predicaments. Armed with a big plate of gingersnaps, I was walking down a long corridor, making my way to a person I had never heard of, let alone ever met.

The deep, rich smell of ginger, cinnamon, and cloves was dizzying to my senses as I clutched the old green and white swirled plate. I wanted to sit in the corner of the hall and eat every single one of those cookies, instead of going by myself to meet someone I did not know.

I walked past a ginormous clock hanging on the wall and thought how very fitting that time is playing such a huge role in this afternoon and in this story. As I continued walking, I thought about how the day had unfolded.

My mother, father, and I were coming home from our annual trip up north to Banff, Alberta, Canada. The weather had been stupendous, the mountain views invigorating, and for each one of us, no clocks existed as time had stood still for five glorious days. We arrived on Sunday for dinner at my grandparents and afterwards I rode my bike, pedaling around the drive and enjoying my grandparent's company.

Monday morning, across the big stones behind Grandpa's little red house, the river was bubbling, and I walked out to see what Grandpa was doing. He said, "Kathy, I think George is home. I better go see him today."

Grandpa and George had been friends for years. I loved how they could look across the river and know if the other was home, seeing if the other was mowing lawn, or picking raspberries. Both of these old men could make each other laugh, talk for hours, and would cross that river in a heartbeat, if the other was in need. George was almost like a brother to Grandpa, but I emphasize that word, *almost*.

Grandpa Neil came from Scottish decent and at one time sported thick red hair and a lot of freckles. As age set it, his hair was more of a dull blonde. He whittled away his days mowing lawns for both of my grandmothers, taking long walks, collecting stray kitties to which Grandma would have no part, and growing things in his garden.

When nighttime fell, Grandpa would pull out his violin and away he would fiddle. He would stomp his feet and ask me to sing. We would have grand old times talking about music and his family.

Grandpa's favorite sibling was the loveable Aunt Maggie. She lived in Montana and each time we would discuss her, he would begin to cry. I tried to avoid that subject as much as I could.

Imagine my surprise when earlier on that Monday morning, I found out Grandpa had a brother still living. Not only was he living, but he lived in the same town in a nearby nursing home. I looked shocked, grabbed a plate full of Grandma's cookies and asked Dad for the keys to the car. I was headed over to meet this uncle I had never heard about.

Mom and Dad insisted on driving me there and on the way filled me in on the whole dreadful family history. It is at this point in my story I would like to relay that utter disappointment and grief overcame me ... mixed with a big dose of embarrassment so that I now can encourage you that *my family* is exactly like *everyone else's*. We have jealousy, betrayal, anger, resentment, and grudges all mixed into the story of our lives.

Apparently, Mom and Dad had visited this uncle several times while I was off gallivanting with the younger cousins. My other grandma, Thelma, knew Grandpa's brother and chatted with him often. What was wrong with me!

The loud voice of a nurse snapped me back to the present and I looked at door number 323; I was almost to room number 360. There it was and the door was partially closed. As I pushed it open ever so gently, I peeked around the corner and saw a man from the back, sitting in his chair, looking out the window. I was in shock. From the back, I could have sworn that my grandpa had come into this room and sat down. I cleared my throat and said, "Excuse me, Uncle Julius?"

The old man turned around slowly and stood up. Again, I was in shock. This extremely tall man was a few years older than Grandpa and looked exactly like him. He had the same dull blonde hair, the same freckles, and the same mannerisms. His face was warm and kind and his eyes twinkled. I could tell that he was so glad to see someone from his family.

We sat down and I explained who I was and then we opened the cookies and began to devour them, me, a young teen, and this sweet old man gobbled down a plate full of gingersnaps *together.*

My folks had dropped me off but promised to come back and pick me up and join me. While they were gone I got caught up on the mystery of this family member I had never known. I finally asked him, "Uncle Julius, why aren't you and Grandpa friends? Why don't you talk?"

I looked at this sweet old man directly in the eyes. Those same blue eyes filled up with tears and I watched them stream down his craggy old face. I grabbed his hand and patted it. It took a moment but he looked at me and said, "You know, I just don't remember. For the life of me, I've tried. I just can't remember why we're mad at each other."

And then it hit me ... *we were just like Joseph's family.* No wonder I loved his story so much. On the way home, Mom and Dad filled me in on the rivalry between the two brothers, including the jealousy, and the resentment. Yet, Uncle Julius, now getting nearer to the end of his life, could not remember why they had a broken relationship.

Grandpa had replaced his brother with a neighbor, his brother had replaced him with others, and their lives went on. But their lives did not go on as God had intended. They went on missing pages and snapshots in the story of what could have made up their lives, because those two siblings were meant to be reconciled.

Webster's Dictionary says that the word, *reconciliation,* means *"the act of causing two people or groups to become friendly again after an argument or disagreement: the process of finding a way to make two different ideas, facts, etc., exist or be true at the same time."*

Pastor John Ortberg says, *"Forgiveness is not just therapeutic or relief*

for the forgiver; it is a loving, humble, repentant quest for reconciliation."

A quest is a long or difficult search for something. Reconciliation means that as a Christ follower, this will not be an easy feat. Forgiving someone will be the first step. Forgetting that sin against you will be the second step. But the third step, reconciliation, the one that makes you want to sit in the corner and eat a plate of gingersnaps, is God asking you to go back to that person with whom you are out of sync, and make things right. Ah, yes, I can hear you groaning as you read those words. God will *never* ask you to do something that He will not provide the help to do, but instead, He will always give you the strength and wisdom to face something difficult when you ask Him for help.

> God will *never* ask you to do something that He will not provide the help to do.

In order to have reconciliation, it will be a lot of work, thus, it is the best choice to try to live in peace with others and to embrace a life free of conflict. But at times, we cannot control what happens, and when trouble or sin separates us, we wonder why we are not in relationship to someone.

The problems within conflict resolution and reconciliation are a bit like hiking up a mountain. **Problem number one** will be facing that person and talking it out. You take a few more steps up the trail.

Problem number two will be the fact that it takes two to work through things. You might show up to a meeting believing that you want restoration and reconciliation, but perhaps that person's heart is still cold and unwilling to resolve anything. You stop and tighten up the boot laces.

Problem number three will be moving past the incident. You take your walking stick, press it into the dirt, and hike to the very top. You begin to look past whatever it was that made you stuck on your path.

Reconciliation is made up of hard work, like hiking up that mountain, not looking back, and reaching the top where life is just a little bit more beautiful and the camera can snap shots of the bigger picture ... resolution, restoration, and reconciliation.

In Genesis 44, we are in the palace with Joseph and his brothers. We left off with them eating their lunch.

The brothers are getting ready to head back to Jacob together. But Joseph needs to do a little further investigation about their attitudes; after all, he wants to know that his full-blood brother, Benjamin is safe and will not meet with the same treachery as Joseph did.

Look Up: Genesis 44:1

"Now Joseph gave these instructions to the steward of his house: 'Fill the men's sacks with as much food as they can carry, and put each man's silver in the mouth of his sack. Then put my cup, the silver one, in the mouth of the youngest one's sack, along with the silver for his grain.'"

Have you ever had someone apologize to you, and continue on with their same bad behavior? I think about my children. So often when they were growing up, I would discipline them for fighting with each other. I would tell them, "Stop picking at your sister this instant and say you are sorry."

One of the siblings would begrudgingly say an unfelt, "Sorry!"

Like clockwork, five minutes would go by and the bad behavior would start all over again! Up the mountain of reconciliation we'd climb!

Joseph is going to take what I like to call a *"pulse check"* on this mountain climb with his brothers. He is trying to find out the truth about their attitudes. Are they truly sorry for their actions? Did they learn anything by being held in a prison, or are they going to snap back with a *"sorry"* and head back to their same old patterns?

The brothers have left the palace now and Joseph gives them just enough time to start on their journey. Joseph has planted a fine silver cup in Benjamin's sack. It was no doubt one of the cups they used for their dinner with Joseph.

 Look Up: Genesis 44:4-5

"They had not gone far from the city when Joseph said to his steward, "'Go after those men at once, and when you catch up with them, say to them, 'Why have you repaid good with evil? Isn't this the cup my master drinks from and also uses for divination? This is a wicked thing you have done.'"

You might wonder what kind of "divination" Joseph is performing. Here is what the Quest Study Bible NIV states, *"This kind of divination was accomplished by placing oil drops upon water and observing the resulting patterns. Divining God's will through dream, the budding of plants, sheep fleeces and the casting of lots was not condemned in the Old Testament. People believed God was totally in control and spoke through these means."*

When confronted, the brothers have no idea what the steward is talking about, and remind him they returned the silver they found. They deny stealing anything and offer a compromise that if anything is found, the Egyptians can take the brother who is harboring the goods, and put him to death. That is how confident they are of their innocence!

Look Up: Genesis 44:12b

"And the cup was found in Benjamin's sack."

The true test of the brother's hearts will now ensue. Scripture tells us that they were so shocked and upset when the silver is found, that they tore their clothes and headed back to the city. Accused of a crime that they did not commit, and at the risk of suffering imprisonment or death, they are beyond afraid. This is sounding a bit too familiar isn't it? After all, being unjustly accused and thrown into prison is Joseph's storyline.

Joseph says that the brother who is found with the stolen cup will stay behind with him. But then a beautiful thing happens! It is the quintessential example of coming full circle. *Judah* offers himself as a replacement for *Benjamin*.

 Look Up: Genesis 44:33

"Now then, please let your servant remain here as my lord's slave in place of the boy, and let the boy return with his brothers."

If you remember, in Genesis 37:26, Judah is the brother who is heading up the sale of slavery of brother, Joseph. Now he offers to become hostage for Benjamin. This shows that the pulse of his heart is now beating repentance, restoration, and resolves not to go down that same path of betrayal that was shown towards Joseph. This was the breaking point for Joseph and he can no longer contain his secrecy over his identity. He sends all of the Egyptians out of the room and the God-planned revelation takes place.

 Look Up: Genesis 45:3

"Joseph said to his brothers, 'I am Joseph! Is my father still living?'"

Can you imagine the shock and the emotions that are running throughout the room? All those years have gone by with anger, guilt, shame, and the task of constantly trying to forget what happened. The same ruler who they are bowing down to, the same one who is giving them food, is the same brother they sold into slavery. Scripture says the brothers were terrified, but Joseph pulls them in close and says do not be distressed.

I believe that the next verses are the most important verses of the entire story.

Look Up: Genesis 45:5-6

"And now, do not be distressed and do not be angry with yourselves for selling me here; because it was to save lives that God sent me ahead of you. For two years no there has been famine in the land, and for the next five years there will not be plowing and reaping."

In the next verse, here lies the purpose of the story of Joseph, because it shows us that God was and is always in charge. God always had the *plan* for Josephs life, God always had the *purpose* for what Joseph was going through, and God always had the *promise* to Joseph that He would never leave him.

Look Up: Genesis 45:7

"But God sent me ahead of you to preserve for you a remnant on earth and to save your lives by a great deliverance. So then, it was not you who sent me here, but God."

The goodness of God is poured out onto the lives of these men. Amidst their bumbling, their cover-up, their hopelessness, God comes through, and lives are changed and saved. God transcends the evil in our lives and a bigger picture is revealed. Even though they sinned, God allowed it because of the greater good for Joseph, for his brothers, and for the Egyptians, Canaanites, and surrounding areas. We are reminded of God's Sovereign hand over our lives in this verse.

Look Up: Proverbs 19:21

"Many are the plans in a man's heart, but it is the Lord's purpose that prevails."

Author and Pastor, John Ortberg had Louis Zamperini, a World War II prison camp survivor, come to his church to speak. Sentenced to a Japanese prison camp, Louis was tortured, routinely beaten, starved, and forced into slave labor.

After the war, Louis moved out of Japan. When he heard a young, Billy Graham, preach a sermon, he gave his life to Christ, and headed back to the place he hated most ... Japan. He ended up at Camp Sugamo, the place that housed 850 prisoners of war, preaching to the same men who beat him. Louis said, *"I thought about tempering the details and emotions, so as not to appear too angry, but I didn't, because otherwise my forgiveness would lack true meaning. I thought this is so profound about how forgiveness is often a long journey, and it will always mean I will have to look at parts of me I didn't think I would have to look at. It will always take courageous honesty. It is different than excusing. Forgiveness means truth about the wrongs done, coming to grips with how I have distorted stuff, as well as other people, because repentance and reconciliation, if they can happen at all, can only happen based on truth."*

Louis experienced something that he never expected. He actually felt compassion for these people who had tormented him. After his talk about God's forgiveness, he jumped off the stage, and down into the crowd. He fell into the arms of those who harmed him, and he repaid that harm with love. He embraced those same men who tortured him. This is the power of our God. This is the ability He has to take evil and turn it into good. This is what happened with Joseph and his brothers. This is the *plan,* the *purpose,* the *promise* of God in our lives ... it is all for God's glory.

Are you in a place today where you don't even remember why you are in conflict with someone? Maybe it's your child and he is mad at you for something you would not let him do, or maybe it is a co-worker who pushed you down trying to get to the top of the corporate ladder, or perhaps it is your own "Uncle Julius," a sibling who you have not spoken to in years.

Whoever it is that you are unreconciled to, it is time to jump off the stage of your life and run into the arms of the one who caused you undue pain. It is time to face them with the love of God and know that God has redeemed us all, and He only allows what is best for the greatest, clearest, most concise picture-perfect print to add to the scrapbook of the story of your life.

Here are some steps that will help when you find the need to reconcile to someone with whom you have a broken relationship.

STEP ONE: *Make the effort to meet* with the person who is in conflict with you.

Hebrews 12:14, *"Make every effort to live in peace with everyone and to be holy; without holiness no one will see the Lord."*

II Corinthians 5:18-19, *"All this is from God, who reconciled us to Himself through Christ and gave us the ministry of reconciliation: that God was reconciling the world to Himself* *in Christ, not counting people's sins against them. And He has committed to us the message of reconciliation."*

Matthew 5:23-24, *"Therefore, if you are offering your gift at the altar and there remember that your brother or sister has something against you, leave your gift there in front of the altar. First go and be reconciled to them; then come and offer your gift."*

STEP TWO: *Assure that person* they are forgiven and you want the relationship to be restored.

Luke 17:3, *"If your brother or sister sins against you, rebuke them; and if they repent, forgive them."*

I Peter 4:8, *"Above all, love each other deeply, because love covers over a multitude of sins."*

II Corinthians 2:7-8, *"Now instead, you ought to forgive and comfort him, so that he will not be overwhelmed by excessive sorrow. I urge you, therefore, to reaffirm your love for him."*

STEP THREE: *Understand that God uses others* to build our character.

Romans 12:14, 16, *"Bless those who persecute you; bless and do not curse. Live in harmony with one another."*

Romans 8:28, *"And we know that all things work together for good to them that love God, to them who are the called according to His purpose."*

Genesis 45:4-5, *"I am your brother Joseph, the one you* *sold into Egypt! And now, do not be distressed and do not be angry with yourselves for selling me here, because it was to save lives that God sent me ahead of you."*

STEP FOUR: *Move past the pain* and do not allow yourself to get pulled back into the cycle of conflict.

Hebrews 12:14, *"Make every effort to live in peace with everyone and to be holy; without holiness no one will see the Lord."*

Isaiah 43:18, *"Forget the former things; do not dwell on the past."*

Philippians 3:13b, *"But one thing I do: Forgetting what is behind and straining toward what is ahead."*

Reconciliation is the main premise of our faith. We are reconciled to God through His Son Jesus Christ, and through the shedding of Jesus' blood on the cross. Jesus has created a bridge between us and God, a bridge of forgiveness and acceptance, a path to the top of the mountain. It is time to make that call, send that email, or knock on that door. It is time to make the hike up the mountain of reconciliation. Embrace the future and move onward and upward!

Steps Recapped:

1. ***Make the effort to meet*** with the person who is in conflict with you.

2. ***Assure that person*** they are forgiven and you want the relationship to be restored.

3. ***Understand that God uses others*** to build our character.

4. *Move past the pain* and do not allow yourself to get pulled back into the cycle of conflict.

📷 **Zoom In:** Although Joseph seemed to be treating his brothers harshly, he was trying to test them and take a true pulse check of their hearts, hoping to discover if they were truly sorry for what they did to him. He set them up to need to return to him by placing a stolen cup in Benjamin's possessions. The same brother, Judah, who pushed to get rid of Joseph, is now the same brother who offers himself up as a replacement for Benjamin. At the end, Joseph overhears the brothers talking and realizes they are truly sorry for what they did. He forgives them, reveals himself to them, and embraces them in true reconciliation.

📷 **Life Lesson Learned:** We learned from Joseph about the art of love and graciousness in the face of those who have harmed us. Instead of placing the blame on his brothers, Joseph gives God credit in allowing the bad to happen and turning it into a life-saving process. Through this part of the story, we see true redemption and are reminded of God's divine plan to allow Jesus to suffer and die for our salvation.

📷 **Questions:**

1. Joseph forgave his brothers completely and embraced them with love. Name a time when you have reconciled with someone who has hurt you.

2. Why do you think Judah was so quick to offer himself as a substitution for Benjamin? Where is God calling you, like Judah, to do something honorable or courageous in your life?

3. Have you ever called someone up to reconcile with them after a considerable amount of time has gone by? What emotions were involved with reconnecting and resolving conflict?

4. Who is in your life right now that you need to reconnect with and try to make amends? What will you do this week to work towards reconciliation?

Look Up:

1. **Proverbs 16:9**

2. **Isaiah 55:8-9**

3. **Jeremiah 10:23**

4. **Romans 8:28**

Songs:

Hymn: "The Old Rugged Cross" *(George Bennard)*
Contemporary: "Jesus Messiah" *(Chris Tomlin)*

Closing Prayer:

Dear Jesus,

It is difficult to get along
with people all the time.

Sometimes the conflict turns
into a broken relationship
and I don't know how to fix it.

Lord help me to make an effort
to reach out to those who are
not in relationship with me.

Help me to be brave and bold
and make the first step to connect.

Help me to embrace that person
and to move onward and upward.

In Jesus' Name, Amen.

CHAPTER 7

Trials to Triumph 📷

Everyone faces adversity; it is an integral part of the life experience. Who you are on the other side of the trial depends on how you face it.

Robyn Carr

📷 **Snapshot:** Last week we learned that God wants us to be reconciled with others and also to Himself. In order to have a life that is full and free, we have to embrace *forgiveness* along with *reconciliation.* Joseph forgave his brothers and reconciled his heart to theirs. That same reconciliation produced redemption for Joseph and his family, and parallels the redemption that Christ provides for each one of us with His death on the cross.

I drove by the house last night. The night was so dark, with a chilly breeze sweeping through my soul as I slowed down and craned my neck to look at it. The backyard, now overgrown with grass and weeds, no longer housed the huge trampoline where my kids spent hours jumping, spinning, and twirling about.

The darkened outline of the house seemed eerie and I felt the same horrific sadness begin to loom over me as it so often does. I pressed my foot to the gas pedal and moved along trying to snuff out the memories and the pain, but not before a few of them came seeping back into my brain.

Thirteen years ago, in the living room of that same house, my children heard the sad words, *"Your dad and I are getting a divorce."* You cannot imagine the screams, the cries, and the horrible hurt that followed those words. I wish I could say that after weeks or years, it has left me. But as you can see from the pain I continue to feel just driving by the house, the pain subsides, but never truly relinquishes its hold on me.

Thinking of those horrible days, I remember being shocked and sickened after a police detective called to inform me about the crystal meth lab that my then-husband and his best friend were running. Add to that some telltale signs of infidelity, and you can understand why I took my children out of the picture of what I had once hoped would be the story of a happy life for all of us.

Days and nights made up the months and years that passed, but the hurts were deep and traveled so far, as though we were in a deep dark pit that we could not escape. Had it not been for the help of my friends, one pastor, a congregation, and many from a small community, I do not know what would have happened. Ultimately God rescued us by using all of those combined individuals.

Each one of my children were thrown with me into this pit of darkness, depression, and devastation. I pleaded with God to release us, send down a huge rope and pull us out, but to no avail. Each one of my girls and I visited a family psychiatrist who tried to paste the brokenness back together, but we could not be fixed.

I cannot tell you how hard it was to walk through the realization that there was no longer a dad to help us. He would not be responsible to us financially, emotionally, physically, or mentally. His anger loomed over each one of our souls and frightened us. For anyone who has walked through divorce by experiencing it themselves, or watching a neighbor, a co-worker, a friend, or a family member go through it, you know how incredibly dreadful it is.

But in due time, after the pit and its blackness had been crafted into a tool that would help develop who we were to become, God came and rescued us. Our heart's cry became this verse: *"Out of my distress I called on the Lord; the Lord answered me and set me free"* (Psalm 118:5). Out of the pit we emerged, but somehow, we seemed held back, as if in a prison of defeat and caution.

Time passed and after several years that same pastor who had become my boss, asked me to consider going on twenty-five dates. How absurd I thought, and yet that request was the key that not only unlocked the prison of my life, but it walked me out into the next phase ... *the palace.*

I agreed to the dates with the promise that after twenty-five, I would be done. I gave each date *(my pastor would screen and approve)* one hour of my time for lunch or breakfast. In that hour, I committed to really caring about that individual, listening to their woes, asking about their family, hearing about their dog, Buster, and then I would bless them and say, "I know that there is someone perfect out there for you, it's not me, so I'll pray for you and I wish you the best." They always seemed to be disappointed, but would graciously accept my decision.

On August 6, date number 24 was a farmer named Dean, who lived out in what I like to term "the middle of nowhere." Forty-three years old and a bachelor that had never been married, he asked himself one day, is there anyone out there for me? Time is flying by and he hadn't had time to meet anyone. He had not been on a date since his early twenties, but suddenly felt like he wanted to try one more time and see if a local dating site would have anyone of interest.

As he searched via zip code, he happened upon a dating site where he saw a picture of a woman outside a Lutheran church, smiling and wearing a jean jacket ... it was me! He sent me a message that said, "If opposites attract, I sure hope we're opposites!"

I responded by asking, "Where in the world is Benson, Minnesota?" He quickly paid his $29.00 and joined so he could answer me. He was date 24 out of 25 *(I had already accepted date number 25, a boring salesman with a big ego)* and I was date number one out of a total of one date for Farmer Dean.

The year of a courtship that followed was one filled with kindness, trust, compassion, and love for my hurting heart and my three hurting girls. When August 6th rolled around again, those three girls and I were in my glorious wedding that gave God the credit, gave friends the accolades, and gave my broken family, the glue it needed to once again be restored. From *the pit* to *the prison* to *the palace.*

The girls and I went through some bumps as we adjusted how we thought about love, trust, faith, and family. And me? Well, I moved out to the *middle of nowhere,* only to find out that the middle of nowhere **was** *somewhere* pretty fabulous.

My life began again the moment I said, "I do," to a man who loved me more than I had ever been loved.

One day, recently, after our nine years of marriage, Farmer Dean was struggling with what he thought was his purpose in life. "I just don't know my purpose. I thought it was to be a farmer, but without my brother and I having any male descendants to take over, there is no one to inherit the farm. I don't think I am doing anything valuable," he said.

We had just finished putting everything away from an event we had

at the little church we own on our farm, and had loaded up the van for another conference for our nonprofit ministry, Best Life. I always try to encourage my husband about how wonderful he is, but I could see that it would be difficult to encourage him through this line of thinking.

After contemplating his purpose, Dean went outside for a minute and I followed him. We sat down on the step and looked out across our corn fields. A huge smile came over his face as he lit up and exclaimed, "Hey! I think I've got it!" He looked directly into my eyes as he spoke. "What if my purpose was to save you from a bad life so you could help save others?" he questioned.

I began to cry. My crying turned to sobs. My husband knew his purpose. It involved redemption, because the same God who left me in *the pit*, came and got me from *the prison*, and placed me on *the palace* floors ... the floors of a farm, a church, a home, a life with this wonderful man, all laid out and established beautifully, in the *middle of somewhere*.

One of my favorite Christian authors, Catherine Marshall says this about trials: *"Of course you'll encounter trouble. But behold a God of power who can take any evil and turn it into a door of hope."*

> God is always about redeeming the bad in our lives. He is constantly working behind the scenes to help us learn, grow, and stretch through the difficulties we encounter.

God is always about redeeming the bad in our lives. He is constantly working behind the scenes to help us to learn, grow, and stretch through the difficulties we encounter.

When we are in the middle of the trials, the triumphs seem out of focus, under developed, or blurry. The camera lens of our souls cannot zoom in on anything good and utter despair can take over. Most of us have been there and we know what that feels like.

Perhaps your wonderful job has been eliminated, your nephew dies of cancer, your daughter moves five hundred miles away, your spouse is unfaithful, or you are diagnosed with a brain tumor.

It is almost as if someone puts the camera lens on the soul of our life and shuts everything down. We cannot think, we cannot move, we cannot breathe. Yet, God is with us and He never leaves us and He is in charge of everything.

Suddenly, we remember that the safety strap that holds the camera around our neck is our hope in the Almighty. The camera represents who God has created us to be. The snapshots are the days we have numbered and God creates them, sees them, and snaps the shot of each glorious moment. Scripture tells us, *"Your eyes saw my unformed body. All the days ordained for me were written in your book before one of them came to be"* (Psalm 139:16).

God has already created the photo album of our lives. The days, the pictures, and the snapshots, He is well aware of everything that is going on, as He allows things to take place for His glory.

We are now in the place in Joseph's story where he is ready to reveal his identity as he pulls his brothers in close and offers them forgiveness, reconciliation, and a comfort he wants them to share.

📷 Look Up: Genesis 45:7

"But God sent me ahead of you to preserve for you a remnant on earth and to save your lives by a great deliverance."

Can you imagine what Joseph and his brothers are thinking as they see God's hand in everything that happened?

Look Up: Genesis 45:8

"So then, it was not you, who sent me here, but God. He made me father to Pharaoh, lord of his entire household and ruler of all Egypt."

Look Up: Revelation 3:7b

"These are the words of Him who is holy and true who holds the key of David. What He opens no one can shut, and what he shuts no one can open."

God opened doors for Joseph that no one else could open. God has allowed Joseph to go through the trials, but He turns them around, just as He will do for us. Out of the darkness, out of the pit, out of the prison, He lifts us up and sets us on a higher plain where triumph comes out of the horrific trials.

Joseph begins to understand the intensity of the complete picture, and is just like anyone of us who wants their parents to be proud of them, he says to his brothers:

Look Up: Genesis 45:13

"'Tell my father about all the honor accorded me in Egypt and about everything you have seen. And bring my father down here quickly.'"

He loved his daddy, Jacob. He wants him to know that he is still alive and that God has done marvelous things since Jacob received that blood soaked coat of many colors and assumed he was dead.

The heart-challenging, mind-stretching, faith-building trials of jealousy, betrayal, rejection, imprisonment, defeat, and abandonment are shed for the new snapshot. We see a picture of a loving brother who has released his anger and pain and relinquishes the old while embracing the new ... a family reconciled to embracing love ... a beautiful new snapshot.

Look Up: Genesis 45:14-15

"Then he threw his arms around his brother Benjamin and wept, and Benjamin embraced him, weeping. And he kissed all his brothers and wept over them. Afterward his brothers talked with him."

The wonderful leader, Joseph, is honored by Pharaoh, and Egypt is pleased that his family is with him. Pharaoh dictates that Joseph's family will come to Egypt and be blessed with food and land.

Look Up: Genesis 45:20

"'Never mind about your belongings, because the best of all Egypt will be yours.'"

It is trial to triumph, flat lined to a pulse, dead to resurrected, underexposed to a perfect print. It is God, the Ultimate photographer, shining His light to make beautiful colors out of inky blackness, and He creates a picture that is more beautifully developed than we ever could imagine.

When the brothers head home to let Jacob know that Joseph is still alive, they travel with money, new clothing, donkeys with grain, bread, and provisions, all provided by Joseph and Pharaoh.

Look Up: Genesis 45:26

"They told him, 'Joseph is still alive! In fact, he is ruler of all Egypt.' Jacob was stunned; he did not believe them. But when they told him everything Joseph had said to them, and when he saw the carts Joseph

had sent to carry him back, the spirit of their father Jacob revived. And Israel (Jacob) said, 'I'm convinced! My son Joseph is still alive. I will go and see him before I die.'"

Trial to triumph all in the hands of God. We watched how God allowed the bad things right alongside the good. We saw how difficult people can affect our story, and how God can redeem it. We understand how important humility is, how desperate jealousy can be, and how imperative it is that one determined, faith-filled person, can change the course of history.

So often in our everyday lives, we want to run from our trials and challenges. We see them as obstacles that get in the way of where we want to go. This story of Joseph shows us a different vantage point, in fact, it is as though we are behind the camera lens taking the pictures of Joseph ourselves.

Here is what we can see clearly: if Joseph did not go to *the pit*, he wouldn't get to *the prison*. If he didn't get to *the prison*, he wouldn't have gotten to *the palace*. If he didn't get to *the palace*, he couldn't save the lives of his family and the many others who experienced the famine. And if he wasn't in charge of Egypt, he could not have saved the family line of Jesus, which comes through Joseph's brother, Judah.

Perhaps you or someone close to you has been going through some intensely difficult trials. Maybe you feel like darkness has surrounded you and you can't seem to pull yourself out of the pit that's engulfed you. There is hope! God allowed Jonah to be in the belly of a big fish, Abraham to prepare his son Isaac as an offering, Esther to face King Xerxes, Noah to face a flood, Moses to face the Red Sea, and Joseph to go to prison.

All of these individuals from the Bible have the same things in common:

1) God was with them.

2) They faced their fears head on.

3) Their risked their lives.

4) God used the trials to build their faith.

God utilized their situation for a great outcome that affected MANY lives in a positive way, and God used the circumstances for His glory. God will do that same thing for you and me, if we choose to trust Him.

Here are some steps that will encourage you to know that all is not lost even though you feel the trials and troubles deeply:

STEP ONE: *Declare to God* that you will remain faith-filled and optimistic.

II Corinthians 4:17, *"For our light and momentary troubles are achieving for us an eternal glory that far outweighs them all."*

Proverbs 23:18, *"There is surely a future hope for you, and your hope will not be cut off."*

Psalm 31:24, *"Be of good courage and He shall strengthen your heart, all ye that hope in the Lord" (KJV).*

STEP TWO: *Stay close to God* through prayer and scripture reading.

📷 **Psalm 119:105,** *"Your Word is a lamp to my feet and a light to my path"(ESV).*

📷 **I Peter 5:7,** *"Casting all your anxieties on Him because He cares for you."*

📷 **Hebrews 4:12,** *"For the word of God is living and active. Sharper than any double-edged sword, it penetrates even to dividing soul and spirit, joints and marrow; it judges thoughts and attitudes of the heart."*

📷 **STEP THREE:** *Wait on God* in the difficult circumstances.

📷 **II Corinthians 4:18,** *"So we fix our eyes not on what is seen, but on what is unseen. For what is seen is temporary, but what is unseen is eternal."*

📷 **James 1:4,** *"Perseverance must finish its work so that you may be mature and complete, not lacking anything."*

📷 **Romans 8:25,** *"But if we hope for what we do not yet have, we wait for it patiently."*

📷 **STEP FOUR:** *Watch for God to move* and see how He redeems the trial to triumph.

📷 **Proverbs 20:24,** *"A person's steps are directed by the Lord. How then can anyone understand their own way?"*

📷 **Psalm 86:11,** *"Teach me your way, Lord, that I may rely on Your faithfulness; give me an undivided heart, that I may fear*

Your name."

Romans 8:28, *"And we know that all things God works for the good of those who love Him, who have been called according to His purpose."*

Trials are a part of life. We will always experience them, but how we respond to them is what really matters. Knowing that God is always in charge, that He is always watching out for your best, and that He alone opens and closes doors is what will give us true peace amidst the trials.

Steps Recapped:

1. **Declare to God** that you will remain faith-filled and optimistic.

2. **Stay close to God** through prayer and scripture reading.

3. **Wait on God** in the difficult circumstances.

4. **Watch for God** to move and see how He redeems the trial to triumph.

Zoom In: Joseph's forgiveness and reconciliation to his brothers is an incredible example to each one of us. He never gave up, he trusted in, and relied on God, and when things came full circle, he threw his arms around his siblings, wept, kissed them, and told them that God allowed the evil to transpire against him, because God was going to use it for a bigger plan. He tells them that God sent him ahead of them to prepare for the famine. Because of Joseph's leadership, the Israelites were saved and the line of Christ was preserved.

Life Lesson Learned: God turns trials into triumphs ... we must learn to trust and embrace the difficulties in our lives because within those troubles will come our deepest life lessons, our best personal growth, and our greatest need for God. If we believe God is with us and in charge of all that happens, we will walk boldly through *the pits, the prisons,* and be ready for *the palace.* After all, for Joseph, that palace really was in the middle of somewhere fabulous.

📷 **Questions:**

1. Joseph realized that God allowed all of the trials for a bigger purpose. Name a time when you went through something difficult and can look back to see it was God's best for you. How did you refocus yourself onto the right path?

2. What lesson do you learn from trials and tribulations? How do you make the choice to become better and not become bitter?

3. What is the first thing you do when a problem occurs? Do you call a friend? Do you talk with your spouse? Do you begin to worry? If you pray, do you typically release the trial to God or do you carry it?

4. Do you struggle with waiting on God? Name a time where you felt God forgot about you. Are you still waiting on Him?

📷 **Look Up:**

1. **Psalm 86:11**

2. **John 16:33**

3. **Romans 12:12**

4. **James 1:12**

📷 **Songs:**

Hymn: "Have Thine Own Way" *(Adelaide A. Pollard & George C. Stebbins)*
Contemporary: "Amazed" *(Jared Anderson)*

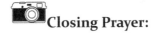**Closing Prayer:**

Dear Jesus,

Help me to trust You at a deeper level.
Help me to understand
that even though trouble will come my way,
You are always in charge of my life.

The pain may be trying, the hardship
challenging, and it may take some time
to get out of *the pit or the prison.*

I can press into You and rely on You completely.
Help me to refuse to be bitter, to focus on Christ,
and remember what is important in life.

Today I pray that You will strengthen my
courage, deepen my faith, and keep me close.
as you prepare the palace for my life.

In Jesus' Name, Amen.

CHAPTER 8

Your Life's Story 📷

Many of life's failures are people who did not realize   how
close they were to success when they gave up.

Thomas Edison

📷 **Snapshot:** Last week we learned that God is the only one who can determine our steps, our pathway, and can open and close doors. At times He will choose to allow difficult circumstances to come into our lives. We might not immediately understand why He allows things, and possibly like Joseph, we will not see His reason for years, if ever, but it brings us comfort to have the knowledge that God is right there with us and is always working behind the scenes to take trials and bring triumph for His glory.

This morning was lovely and fall-like, as I sat down in the comfort of my big leather chair, coffee cup grasped in one hand and Bible in the other. I looked out the window at the golden leaves that were swirling down from a big tree and remembered a morning that was as bright and sunny as this one. I hated those moments in time where the snapshot of my old life would settle into the frame of my mind and try to take over my emotions. But for a moment today, I let myself travel back to that time in life when days were desperate and my life's story was almost altered in a different direction.

Many years ago it had felt like that same fall-like day, with crisp breezes blowing, and yellow, red, and brown leaves dancing through the bright sunny sky. Yet, I could not find it within myself to feel the joy and light the sunshine was trying to permeate.

I had just hung up the phone from another trying episode between myself and my children's father. His shouting penetrated the receiver against my ear and frightened my spirit. I had no idea how to handle his angry spells and our fragile relationship was quickly deteriorating.

His threats, accusations, and anger were starting to weigh heavily on my spirit and I felt myself faltering. He hissed into the phone, "I will make sure you lose your job. I will keep any church from ever hiring you. When they find out that you divorced a drug addict who needed help, they'll never want you. No one will ever want you. No one will ever love you. You will never be free of me!" he exclaimed. I hung up the phone and trembled. I felt shaken to the core and very alone.

A feeling of fatigue and hopelessness took over. I felt desolate and helpless. Even though I knew that the lies he had been sharing were ridiculous, within a co-dependent relationship one begins to believe the lies. My mind snapped that morning and I began to carry the burden that I would never have another worship director position, I would parent alone, and I would always be alone. Those words, "You'll never be free of me," terrified me, not just because it was a threat, but because I believed them.

I called my father and began to recite a simple plan. "I can't go through with the divorce. It's been almost twenty years of marriage. The police will come here, they will find his drugs hidden, my children will be taken to foster care, and I will slip slowly back into the pit. I cannot compete with his drugs and the violence anymore. I feel myself sinking," I told my father. "I'm hanging up now. I don't know how to go on. I cannot get myself out of this." I hung up the phone.

I sat staring out at the leaves falling from the trees and fifteen minutes later, there was a knock at my door. My best friend was there with a steaming hot cup of coffee and a big blanket. She sat me down in my leather chair and covered me, speaking calmly, quietly, as though I could hear and understand her. But, I could not.

Fifteen more minutes went by as the clock chimed on the half hour and another ring came at the door. Another friend had sent her husband and child over. Her husband walked in and put his hand on my shoulder and prayed. I felt oblivious to what was going on as if I was in a trance.

The ring of the phone pierced the still room as I answered and heard the voice of my former pastor. He spoke quietly, ever so gently and said, "Kath, listen to my words and start to focus on them. Christ is with you. He's never left you. This is the part of the journey where God sees what you are made of and He challenges you to step into that life that is meant for you. This part of your story is not the end ... it is just the beginning. Can you hear me? You must get up and walk out. This isn't about people telling you that you can't leave a poor drug addict, this is about police and danger and the law. You must get your children and yourself out of that house and quickly."

The urgency of his voice snapped me out of the blurriness controlling my brain and I heard his last words to me as he said, "You are going to let the people in this room pray over you right now. You are going to get up and walk out of this place and you will never look back. You will never second guess yourself. You were made to be a mother, made to be a worship director, and made to walk in freedom."

The strength of those friends and their prayers saved my life that day, and all because one 75-year-old father hung up the phone from his distraught daughter and frantically called his child's friends and her pastor for help since he lived nine hours away. Dad knew that my call was a call of desperation. I had lost my way. I had forgotten who God had made me to be. I was back in *the pit* and headed for *the prison*.

Days later, as my head cleared, I began to think about how God had wired my personality, my gifts and talents, and how He had arranged for me to grow in my skill level. I remembered how it started at age four. I settled into a church pew next to my father and pointed to the woman with the big beehive hairdo playing the old upright piano. "Someday, Daddy, I'll play piano like that," I said. After church that day, I asked my daddy who would tell people about Jesus.

Dad responded by saying, "You will, Kathleen. As long as you're alive, your job will be to tell people about Jesus."

At age twelve, our pastor handed me a hymnal and said, "There is no one to play piano for us, Kathy. Tag ... you're it!"

From that moment on I embraced my piano lessons *(Mom made a deal with me that I didn't have to help with dishes if I'd just practice)*, and worked on practicing hymns. Mrs. Linkee, my piano teacher charged seventy five cents a lesson for the 13 years I took lessons! I planned and led all the worship services each Sunday morning, evening, and Wednesday for the next 38 years. It was who God had intended me to be.

Now, because of the evil of someone else, I was thrown into a prison of control, anger, and sin. I waited and wondered, but I **never doubted** one thing ... *who God wanted me to be.* I knew that the gifts He gave me were made up of leadership, music, organization, prayer, and a desire to let people know that Jesus died for them. It all fit nicely into a snapshot of ministry, and in ministry, I continued to serve! I did walk out of that imprisonment that day with fall leaves dropping from the tree outside. I did walk into freedom. I did get another job as a worship director where I was loved and encouraged, and God redeemed my famine of

love and support through a wonderful husband named Dean.

Sometimes it is very obvious who God has created us to be. We love to teach, to sing, to assist others, or we love medicine, science, or nature. Each one of us is created uniquely for a purpose and a plan. God uses all of us to fit together, serving one another, like a giant family portrait.

At other times, we are not sure what we want to do, and we question God, ourselves, and others, desperately trying to figure things out.

Joseph's plan was to be a shepherd with his brothers. He assumed he would be a leader in his family and continue on the same path he was traveling, but because of others, he was sidetracked. It is in this part of Joseph's story that we can realize again, that God may have created Joseph to be a shepherd for that time in his life, but God was grooming Joseph's leadership and allowed the bad to happen so Joseph could grow and be transformed into something even better than he imagined. Still a shepherd of sorts, leading people, he was refined. God developed Joseph's leadership skills, fine tuned his gifts of dream interpretation, tweaked his pride, strengthened his morals, and gave Him the wisdom, determination, and vision to lead an entire country as well as those around him during a seven year famine.

God knew all along that Joseph had those gifts deep in his personality, but Joseph could have listened to the voices that said, "I will make sure no one ever hires you, no one will love you, no one will want you," but he didn't. Who was there to encourage Joseph? God. Who was there to

> At other times, we are not sure what we want to do, and we question God, ourselves, and others, desperately trying to figure things out.

emphatically remind him of who he was? God. Who was there to get him back on track to become who he was meant to be and walk in freedom? God.

Dr. Orison Swett Marden says this about our journey: *"The Creator has not given you a longing to do what you have no ability to do."*

At times we will arrange the photos we want to take for our life's story. We will put people and things in their place and have them pose where we think they should be, only to find out that life is not that simple. Things happen that will distract us from the path God has set us on. We can end up someplace questioning ourselves, discouraged, down and out, and out of focus.

Notice in Joseph's story, scripture does not report any doubt within his spirit. His attitude remains faithful to God no matter the consequences. Would we react the same?

I read about a man who was similar to Joseph. He had great gifts from God and his own well-posed picture of life. He set out on the path he supposed was right, but others affected that plan.

- In his twenties, he failed in a business twice, was defeated for the legislature and had a nervous breakdown.

- In his thirties, he was defeated for Congress, was later elected to Congress and later was defeated for Congress again.

- In his forties, he was defeated for the Senate and for the office of Vice President.

- However, at 51, he was elected President of the United States.

His name? Abraham Lincoln. Just like Joseph, God was in charge of what he would do, where he would go, how defeat would propel him and how he would change a nation. Will we remain faithful when people and things get in our way?

Our lives are not picture perfect. Obstacles and injustices can alter our story. Joseph's story didn't go *according to **his** plan,* but God had it go *according to **His** plan.*

Matthew Henry says: *"Cast not away your confidence because God defers his performances. That which does not come in your time, will be hastened in his time, which is always the more convenient season. God will work when he pleases, how he pleases, and by what means he pleases. He is not bound to keep our time, but he will perform his word, honor our faith, and reward them that diligently seek him."* What a wonderful encouragement for our souls!

We are now in the place in Joseph's story where Joseph sends for his father, Jacob, to join him. Joseph tells his family what to say when they are presented to Pharaoh.

📷 **Look Up: Genesis 47:1**

"Joseph went and told Pharaoh, 'My father and brothers, with their flocks and herds and everything they own, have come from the land of Canaan and are now in Goshen.'"

The brothers tell Pharaoh they are shepherds and Pharaoh blesses Joseph's family.

📷 **Look Up: Genesis 47:5-6a**

"Pharaoh said to Joseph, 'Your father and your brothers have come to you, and the land of Egypt is before you; settle your father and your brothers in the best part of the land. Let them live in Goshen ...'"

This was an instance of Pharaoh showing his gratitude to Joseph for his superb leadership. They are to settle in *the best part of the land.* He offers Joseph's family the preferential treatment and asks them to shepherd Pharaoh's livestock.

Look Up: Genesis 47:6b

"And if you know of any among them with special ability, put them in charge of my own livestock."

I love the impact that Joseph has on the people of Egypt, Canaan, and the surrounding areas. Because they are experiencing a famine, Joseph collected money for the grain that people were buying. But when all their money was gone, Joseph needed to come up with a new plan. Everything that he was created to do and all of his experience through the years at the prison are helping him to be a great leader in the palace. How could he have planned for this?

Look Up: Genesis 47:15

"When the money of the people of Egypt and Canaan was gone, all Egypt came to Joseph and said, 'Give us food. Why should we die before your eyes? Our money is used up.'"

Joseph bought all of their land and gave them seed to plant.

Look Up: Genesis 47:23

"Joseph said to the people, 'Now that I have bought you and your land today for Pharaoh, here is seed for you so you can plant the ground. But when the crop comes in, give a fifth of it to Pharaoh. The other four-fifths you may keep as seed for the fields and as food for yourselves and your households and your children.'"

Kind, supportive, and business-minded, Joseph leads the people through famine and difficult times, just as God had led him through a famine of sorts in his own life. God protects the Israelites, knowing all along that a famine would occur and keeps them safe, sends them to Egypt where one of their own, an Israelite, is the leader.

Look Up: Genesis 47:27

"Now the Israelites settled in Egypt in the region of Goshen. They acquired property there and were fruitful and increased greatly in number."

Salvation to the Israelites came in the form of a simple seventeen year old shepherd, betrayed by his brothers, sold as a slave, thrown into prison and walking the floors of a palace. If he was not sent on ahead, the Israelites would have been snuffed out and there would have been no Judah to continue the lineage of Jesus Christ, Savior of the world. God had a plan and what a plan it was!

Today you may be experiencing doubts and questions about your own life story. Perhaps you are uncertain of your own purpose in life or where your story will take you. Maybe you are wondering how you can help others or what you can do to serve and make a difference. Maybe you don't think your gifts are valuable, but God has made you and I, and in His eyes we ARE valuable!

We can safely assume that Joseph's plan was just to stay home and be a good shepherd. Inside his heart and soul, he was created to become a great leader. I am sure he thought he had the whole picture in the frame, but some of the photo was cut off. God made his story a unique scrapbook of photos. God took Joseph's gifts, grew and matured them, and used him at a much deeper level to change history. God wants you to be living out the gifts He's given to you and He wants you to live your best life.

📷 **Look Up: John 10:10b**

"I have come that they may have life and have it to the full."

Here are some steps that will encourage you to look deep inside your own heart and soul and see how God is leading you to have life to the fullest:

📷 **STEP ONE:** *Discover the gifts and desires in your heart,* bring them to the surface and write them down.

> 📷 **Psalm 37:4,** *"Take delight in the Lord, and He will give you the desires of your heart."*

> 📷 **Proverbs 3:5-8,** *"Trust in the Lord with all your heart and lean not on your own understanding. In all your ways submit to Him and He will make your paths straight."*

> 📷 **Psalm 139:13-16,** *"For You created my inmost being; You knit me together in my mother's womb. I praise You because I am fearfully and wonderfully made; Your works are wonderful, I know that full well. My frame was not hidden from You when I was made in the secret place, when I was woven together in the depths of the earth. Your eyes saw my unformed body; all the days ordained for me were written in Your book before one of them came to be."*

📷 **STEP TWO:** *Seek God* for His will for your life's story.

> 📷 **James 4:8a,** *"Come near to God and He will come near to you ..."*

> 📷 **Deuteronomy 4:29,** *"But if from there you seek the Lord*

your God, you will find Him if you seek Him with all your heart and with all your soul."

📷 **I Chronicles 16:11,** *"Seek the Lord and His strength, seek His presence continually" (ESV).*

📷 **STEP THREE:** *Pray, meditate and seek wise counsel* to help you begin to realize your potential and purpose.

📷 **Philippians 4:6-7,** *"Do not be anxious about anything, but in every situation, by prayer and petition, with thanksgiving, present your requests to God. And the peace of God, which transcends all understanding, will guard your hearts and your minds in Christ Jesus."*

📷 **Joshua 1:8,** *"Keep this Book of the Law always on your lips; meditate on it day and night, so that you may be careful to do everything written in it. Then you will be prosperous and successful."*

📷 **Proverbs 12:15,** *"The way of a fool is right in his own eyes, but a wise man listens to advice."*

📷 **STEP FOUR:** *Take tangible steps to attain the dream* God has placed in your heart.

📷 **Ephesians 2:10,** *"For we are God's handiwork, created in Christ Jesus to do good works, which God prepared in advance for us to do."*

📷 **Ephesians 5:1-2,** *"Follow God's example, therefore, as dearly loved children and walk in the way of love, just as Christ loved us and* *gave Himself up for us as a fragrant offering and sacrifice to God."*

Romans 12:1, *"Therefore, I urge you, brothers and sisters, in view of God's mercy, to offer your bodies as a living sacrifice, holy and pleasing to God—this is your true and proper worship."*

Becoming who God wants us to be is about figuring out how He has made us. When we ask the Holy Spirit to help us look through the zoom lens on the camera of our life and look closely at our talents, interests, and desires, we can begin to understand the whole picture of who we really are and who God wants us to be.

John Ortberg says, *"When the Spirit flows in you, you are given power to become the person God designed. You become you-ier."*

It's time to get focused on your purpose and plan and begin to fill the pages of your story with snapshots of your life ... real life ... a better life!

Steps Recapped:

1. *Discover the gifts and desires in your heart,* bring them to the surface and write them down.

2. *Seek God* for His will for your life's story.

3. *Pray, meditate and seek wise counsel* to help you begin to realize your potential and purpose.

4. *Take tangible steps to attain the dream* God has placed in your   heart.

Zoom In: The desires held in Joseph's heart, his training, and his abilities led him on a path that would serve God. God creates unique gifts and talents in each one of us and wants us to use those gifts to serve Him. Each life is valuable and each life has a purpose. It is our job to find those gifts and use them for His purpose.

Life Lesson Learned: Frequently in life, when we think things are too difficult and we can't go on, that is exactly the time when God comes in and helps us turn the corner on the situation. When we seek God for our purpose and His plan, we will find Him, and I guarantee you, it will be the best plan with the most perfect camera, developing the most beautiful pictures, you could ever take!

Questions:

1. When Joseph started out as a shepherd he had no idea of his life's future story. Name three things a shepherd does that would help Joseph with his future leadership role.

2. What gifts and talents has the Lord given to you? Are you currently using those gifts to encourage others ? If yes, give one example of using your gifts in a public setting and one example from a private setting.

3. Do you believe you are living your life to the fullest? If not, what is holding you back? What could you do today to live your best life?

4. God is in control of the camera and the pictures are being taken, as your life unfolds before you. Name one thing you will do this week to seek God about His plan and purpose for your life's story.

Look Up:

1. Proverbs 18:16

2. Romans 12:6

3. I Corinthians 12:4-6

4. I Peter 4:10-11

Songs:

Hymn: "Take My Life and Let It Be" *(Frances Havergal and H.A. Cesar Malan)*
Contemporary: "Everyday" *(Joel Houston)*

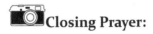**Closing Prayer:**

Dear Jesus,

Please reveal to me the gifts
that You have created inside of me.

Help me to realize Your desire
for my life and to know how
I can use those gifts to serve You
and to help others.

Just as Joseph was able
to grow in his skill level,
I pray that You will help me
to keep growing in mine.

Give me a desire to live
my life to the fullest.

In Jesus' Name, Amen.

Conclusion
The Story of My Life: Joseph 📷

There are no disappointments to those whose
wills are buried in the will of God.

Frederick William Faber

📷 **Snapshot:** Last week we learned that God has created each one of us with unique gifts and talents that we are to use to serve Him and to encourage others. Joseph's gifts began at a young age when he was shepherding his flock, but because of difficult circumstances that God allowed Him to walk through, Joseph's gifts were refined and he was able to do more than feed and care for sheep, he was gifted to feed and care for people!

Life seemed pretty wonderful for me, with a worship director's position, a growing women's ministry that was created out of the troubles my girls and I had experienced, a great husband, a lovely farm, and wonderful friends and family. I felt like palace-living was now mine.

But as time went by, the seventy minute job commute in snow, the change of lead staff, and a stirring desire to do more for God, left me in a quandary. I could feel a slight push of God within my restless spirit but refused to look at it with a zoom lens on the camera of my life.

Each week for four years, I had told my husband that I saw a small white building in his grove, south of our farm, next to our home. Each week my husband laughed at me and said, "I'm not having any buildings on my land. I'm a farmer! Our land is sacred."

Day after day I focused my sight on the little white 1890's schoolhouse across the road from our farm. I would make the long drive home from the church and see that building and think, maybe that is where our women's ministry headquarters should be. I love old buildings, old architecture, old songs, old people! Our ministry was coming up on five years and I thought it was time to have something that made a statement, someplace that said, "This is our home."

I would pray and wait, and wait and pray. Until finally one day I felt similar to Joseph because I was no longer called to shepherd the same flock. No, God was developing in me a different kind of leadership, and unique skill sets were being refined. With a sad heart and a reluctant spirit, I resigned from my church position and went full time to my women's ministry. It was scary to say the least!

After several months, a stirring in my heart and soul was so frantic I knew I had to move or would miss out on what God wanted me to do. I just wasn't sure, so I started by pulling out my camera and looking around for the next picture God wanted as part of my life story.

My dear neighbor, Mona, invited me for coffee. That morning, her sister-in-law, LuElla, joined us and I cast a vision for the women's ministry at the little schoolhouse. I knew it was quaint, close, and old, so I believed it would be the perfect place to set up headquarters. Those friends prayed with me, encouraged me, and cheered me on.

A week later, Mona invited another neighbor, JaVonne, for coffee and I joined them only to cast my vision to her as well. We prayed again about the little building. They encouraged me onward.

After talking with my husband, Dean, he agreed to meet with the town board to see if they would rent the old schoolhouse. We anxiously held hands and crossed the street that Tuesday night to meet with the board, only to have them say no. I would have been devastated except when I got into the schoolhouse that night, I did not feel the pleasure of God. I could not see the ministry in the building. Something wasn't right!

Each time we would drive on the highway in front of our home, Dean and I would pray for our community and the surrounding areas. We prayed God would provide three things for us as a ministry: an entry way, an area that would hold conferences and Bible studies, and a kitchen. We looked in a nearby town, but everything was too expensive to rent. I am happy to be married to a smart business-minded farmer who figures things out and said it was too costly to rent. He thought we would need to buy a building.

After a couple of weeks into our search, the farmer that lives behind us (from the town board) called and said, "I think you should look for an old church." The thought had never crossed our minds! We began to talk about where we would find an old church for sale. How far away would it be? What would it cost? The next afternoon, the farmer that lives across the road from us called and said, "I've been praying for you two and I think you should look for an old church to buy." That was it, it was confirmation from God to look for an old church. We prayed about it that night and thought the next morning, we would get to work with our church search.

That was at 8:00 p.m. on Tuesday night, two weeks after the town board turned us down. At 8:00 a.m. on Wednesday morning, twelve hours later, my husband called and exclaimed, "You'll never believe what's on the front page of the paper!"

"What?" I questioned.

"A church for sale. And Kathy ... it's old! It's from 1900."

"What? Where!!! I'm driving there right now. Wait! How much is it?"

And then my husband answered with the most wonderful news ever ... *"It's on Craigslist for $1.00."*

My sister-in-law went with me and as I drove up and walked through the front doors, into an entry way, into a sanctuary, and then into a roughed-in kitchen, I looked at the tin ceilings, awed over the stained glass, smiled at the old oak bead board and held back everything within my soul that was telling me to burst out in tears, do a little jig and shout Hallelujah!

Frank Lake Covenant Church, built in 1900 for $2000.00, had sat empty for thirty years. The ministry that had occurred there had taken to rest, but its work was not complete. I breathed in a silent prayer to God and asked the kind gentleman who was selling the church if he wanted his dollar right then.

I knew one thing in that moment in time, that God had provided something so much better than my plan, but I still had one dilemma ... how to convince the farmer who would not give up his grove.

Interestingly enough, when Dean bought his property, an old house had been in the south grove and once it was torn down, nothing would grow. Dean had planted various trees, bushes, flowers, grass, but still, it was an empty spot. In my mind, I believed the little white church was supposed to be there.

When my husband arrived at the old church, he acted calm while measuring and taking notes. He said, "I'll have to see how things fit," and we drove home. We walked out to the grove and Dean began to measure things. He looked up at me in surprise and said, "I would never have believed it to be true! The size of the church is exactly the size where nothing will grow!" I began to cry, but it was not resolved yet. The farmer would have to relinquish the land, and my farmer loved his grove.

I prayed throughout the night, but I knew enough about my relationship with God and Dean, that I would need to let God take charge, and as a leader who was more importantly a wife, I would have to agree with whatever my husband decided. As he opened his eyes that next morning, he looked right at me and said, "I know what we are supposed to do. We are moving that church twenty miles to our grove and we will have headquarters for the ministry. What are the chances that thirty years have gone by where it has sat empty and now when we are looking, it's available! God has designed all of this for right now and we need to go with it!"

If I would have remained in the pit of despair and abuse, I would have missed the opportunity of my position at the church that helped me and the girls. If I had allowed myself to stay in the prison of shame, divorce, and guilt of single parenting, I would have never met Farmer Dean. If I had stayed as the worship director, I would have missed that day when the church was for sale for $1.00. I was the fourth person who called and several were interested in moving the building.

Thirty years had gone by where that church sat empty. Thirty-eight years went by where I served as a worship director, but when it was the right time, God's time, our church was available. It was affordable, it was beautiful, it was everything we ever wanted ... *and so much more.*

God is in the business of transforming lives and situations to bring the best to us when we wait on Him, remain faithful, and watch for His hand to move. When we think we cannot go on, when we cannot see our way, when we cannot figure it out, when everything is going wrong, that is when we need to listen for God's voice because He *will* come into the picture at just the right time, with just the right setting, just

> God is in the business of transforming lives and situations to bring the best to us when we wait on Him, remain faithful, and watch for His hand to move.

the right lighting, and exactly the right angle of the camera lens. He sees the entire picture and knows how to make things better! He gives us the desires of our heart at a deeper level than we can ever imagine!

 Look Up: Psalm 21:2

"You have granted him his heart's desire and have not withheld the request of his lips."

It must have been scary and unsettling for Joseph to be cast into a deep pit and then sold into slavery. Once he served Potiphar and was thrown into prison, that fear must have returned, but he pushed past fear and remained confident in God, his helper.

Author A.W. Tozer says this about God: *"We need never shout across the spaces to an absent God. He is nearer than our own soul, closer than our most secret thoughts."* There is no shame in questions, no guilt in wondering, no harm in being scared. There is however, peace where there is faith.

Notice in Joseph's story, scripture does not report any doubt within his spirit. His attitude remains faithful to God no matter the consequences. Would we react the same?

In Joseph's story, God saves the best for last. It is as though we were able to see the picture being snapped, but we have been waiting for the print to be developed. We are now in the place in Joseph's story where his father, Jacob, dies. Joseph's brothers began to get fidgety. They worry that without Jacob there to keep Joseph accountable, they

will experience ramifications for their prior horrific sin against their brother.

 Look Up: Genesis 50:15-17

"When Joseph's brothers saw that their father was dead, they said, 'What if Joseph holds a grudge against us and pays us back for all the wrongs we did to him?' So, they sent word to Joseph, saying, 'Your father left these instructions before he died: 'This is what you are to say to Joseph: I ask you to forgive your brothers the sins and the wrongs they committed in treating you so badly,' Now please forgive the sins of the servant of the God of your father." When their message came to him, Joseph wept."

A little discernment will tell you that there is some guilt mixed with manipulation in this plea. Dad is dead, Dad says you have to forgive us because we serve God and you loved Dad. But Joseph doesn't take offense, instead, his kind heart weeps for the loss of his father and for the desperation of his brothers. Joseph sees their manipulation, he hears the fear within their words. Yet, Joseph remains faithful to God and is who God has made him to be ... a good leader.

 Look Up: Genesis 50:18

"His brothers then came and threw themselves down before him. 'We are your slaves,' they said."

Again, Joseph and his brothers are reminded of the beginning of the story of Joseph ... the dreams. They are once again bowing down before their brother. But Joseph doesn't lord his leadership over them, he loves them, he forgives them, and he sees the bigger picture.

 Look Up: Genesis 50:19-21

"But Joseph said to them, 'Don't be afraid. Am I in the place of God? You

intended to harm me, but God intended it for good to accomplish what is now being done, the saving of many lives. So then, don't be afraid. I will provide for you and your children.' And he reassured them and spoke kindly to them."

They didn't deserve it, did they? In these simple verses, in this heartfelt statement, we see a parallel to Jesus Christ. As He hung on the cross, He could have said the same words to His betrayers. *"You intended to harm me, but God intended it for good to accomplish what is now being done, the saving of many lives."* **God allowed the *bad* to happen so that *more good* than *bad* would happen.**

The story continues to come back to *several key life lessons* we can learn from Joseph.

📷 1. *People with bad intentions are continually used to push and propel us* to where God needs us to be. Very often, we would find ourselves with the same complacent attitude if we did not get a shove along the way. The Hebrew word for prosperity is *prospérité* meaning to "push forward."

📷 2. *Each individual's life is valuable to God.* He has a plan and a purpose for all of us. He has given each one of us gifts and talents that are hard wired into our beings. It is our job to find those talents, foster them, and use them for God's glory to encourage and help others.

📷 3. *We must always give God credit.* Joseph never took the glory for himself, but continually gave God the credit. God blessed Joseph, his family, and Pharaoh for Joseph's right heart before God.

📷 4. *We must remain faithful even when the times are difficult.* God is always in the situation with us, and He is God and we are NOT!

📷 5. *Bad things will happen to good people.* It is inevitable. We live in a sinful world so evil exists and bad things happen. Why would we think that we would be excluded from trouble?

▣ **6. *God never leaves us.*** No one will ever know you better or love you more than Creator God. He needs us to trust Him. He is wise, loving, and always looking out for our best.

▣ **7. *We make our plans for our own story, but God creates a better plan.*** God can completely turn things around even when we have made a big mess of things, or when others have made a disaster of our lives. His ways are always better!

▣ **8. *God's timing is perfect.*** When we do not understand why God is not answering our prayers, giving us a job, sending us a spouse, giving us something that we think is crucial, we must rely on God's infinite wisdom that His ways and His timing are perfect. He orchestrates things to work out for the bigger picture.

Joseph suffered for a while. *The pit* is darkness, suffering, loss, rejection, betrayal. He went to Potiphar's and then to captivity. *The prison* held Joseph down with thoughts of death, hopelessness, darkness, and loss. But God rescued him and he found himself in charge of the palace. *The palace* is freedom, happiness, and prosperity where Joseph and you are set free to use God given gifts, talents, and skills to serve as the Lord intended. People learn from us when we are in the pits and prisons. We learn from others when they are there. But most of all, we learn about ourselves, our faith, and our God when we are in the darkest parts of our life's story.

▣ **Look Up: I Peter 1:6-7**

"For a little while you have had to suffer great and all kinds of trials. These have come so that your faith may be proved genuine and may result in praise, glory and honor when Jesus Christ is revealed."

Here are some steps that will encourage you to believe that no matter what your trials are, no matter who has hurt you, been jealous of you, betrayed you, or over looked you, God sees you, knows you, loves you, and wants you to believe that you are valuable. He has a purpose and a plan for your life:

STEP ONE: *Look back to see God's FORGIVENESS.*

I John 1:9, *"If we confess our sins, He is faithful and just and will forgive us our sins and purify us from all unrighteousness."*

Psalm 25:18, *"Look on my affliction and my distress and take away all my sins."*

Hebrews 8:12, *"For I will forgive their wickedness and will remember their sins no more."*

STEP TWO: *Look back to see God's FAITHFULNESS.*

Lamentations 3:22-23, *"Because of the Lord's great love we are not consumed, for His compassions never fail. They are new every morning; great is Your faithfulness."*

Psalm 91:4, *"He will cover you with His feathers, and under His wings you will find refuge; His faithfulness will be your shield and rampart."*

II Thessalonians 3:3, *" But the Lord is faithful, and He will strengthen you and protect you from the evil one."*

📷 **STEP THREE:** *Look now to see God's PROVISION.*

📷 **Psalm 111:5,** *"He provides food for those who fear Him; He remembers His covenant forever."*

📷 **Deuteronomy 28:12,** *"The Lord will open the heavens, the storehouse of His bounty, to send rain on your land in season and to bless all the work of your hands. You will lend to many nations but will borrow from none."*

📷 **II Corinthians 9:10,** *"Now He who supplies seed to the sower and bread for food will also supply and increase your store of seed and will enlarge the harvest of your righteousness."*

📷 **STEP FOUR:** *Look ahead to see God's PROMISES.*

📷 **Matthew 11:28-29,** *"Come to me, all you who are weary and burdened, and I will give you rest. Take my yoke upon you and learn from me, for I am gentle and humble in heart, and you will find rest for your souls."*

📷 **Philippians 4:19,** *"And my God will meet all your needs according to the riches of His glory in Christ Jesus."*

📷 **Romans 8:37,** *"No, in all these things we are more than conquerors through Him who loved us."*

I love the quote from pastor and theologian, John Wesley, *"Do all the good you can. By all the means you can. In all the ways you can. In all the places you can. At all the times you can. To all the people you can. As long as ever you can."*

There is purpose in our lives. There is a path and a plan. When we are uncertain, we go to God in faith. When we are afraid, we go to God in prayer. When we are rescued, we go to God in gratefulness. Each life is valuable. Each person is created in the image of God. What's your plan? What's your purpose? There is always purpose in the pain.

Steps Recapped:

1. *Look back to see God's FORGIVENESS.*

2. *Look back to see God's FAITHFULNESS.*

3. *Look now to see God's PROVISION.*

4. *Look ahead to see God's PROMISES.*

Zoom In: God has placed specific desires in our heart. When we daily seek Him for forgiveness, direction, provision and claim His promises, we watch and see how faithful God is throughout the pages of our story. Our eyes can only see a small viewpoint through the camera lens of our hearts and minds, but God always has the big picture in mind and it is full of His best prints for you and me!

Life Lesson Learned: Joseph's trouble had purpose. God does not waste opportunities to help us and make something good out of something bad. It seems fairly simple when we look at God's Word. Follow Him. Follow His call. Take His lead. Pick up your camera. Chase after the scary and challenging. Face your fears. Remain faithful. Discover who you are and who God wants you to be. *Because when you do ... the scariest things can certainly become the most wonderful God-opportunities.* Take the picture! Take the picture!

📷 Questions:

1. Joseph had the opportunity to pay his brother's back for their sins against him, and yet, his heart was soft and he loved them. Name a time in your life when you could have turned your back on someone, but you chose to forgive?

2. God is on your side! He directs your camera angles and works in ways that you might not have anticipated. Name a time when you experienced things falling into place and knew it was God's hand working through the camera of your life.

3. Looking back through the years gives us insight on how God challenges us to grow our personalities, and we see our weak spots where the enemy attacks us. Write about a time when you experienced God challenging you to grow.

4. Joseph had negative influences in his life, but was able to have a positive outcome. Is there someone in your life who has tried to affect you negatively, but it made you a better person? If so, how did God use that incident to develop your character? Share how you were able to remain in Godly focus.

Look Up:

1. Deuteronomy 31:6

2. Psalm 59:16-17

3. Psalm 147:11

4. Philippians 4:13

Songs:

Hymn: "Savior Like a Shepherd Lead Us" *(Dorothy A. Trupp and William B. Bradbury)*
Contemporary: "Never Let Go" *(Matt Redman)*

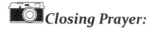

Closing Prayer:

Dear Jesus,

Thank you for the lessons
I can learn from Joseph.

He loved You, loved his family,
was faithful, held strong morals,
forgave easily, worked hard,
and helped others with his gifts and talents
And he gave You the glory.

Help me to implement those
characteristics into my own heart.

Help me to know
that nothing can happen to me
without Your knowledge,
Your will, and Your care.

I praise You for creating me
just the way I am.
Help me to find my gifts
and use them for Your glory.

In Jesus' Name, Amen.

 Resources

Introduction

1. Emerson, Ralph Waldo. Web. [http://www.goodreads.com/quotes/64541-the-purpose-of-life-is-not-to-be-happy-it].

2. Pink, A. W. "Providence Baptist Ministries." Web. [http://www.pbministries.org/books/pink/Gleanings_Genesis/genesis.htm].

Chapter 1

* Names Changed

1. Penn, William. "The Quote Garden." Web. [http://www.quotegarden.com/jealousy.html].

2. *Merriam Webster's Collegiate Dictionary, 11th Edition.* Springfield, MA: Merriam-Webster, Inc., 2009.

3. Ortberg, John. "My Favorite Hero: Joseph." Web. July 8-9, 2006. [http://data.mppc.org/sermon/transcript/060709_jortberg].

4. Stone, Oliver. "Brainy Quote." Web. [http://www.brainyquote.com/quotes/quotes/o/oliverston311017.html].

5. Moore, Beth. *Get Out of That Pit.* Nashville, TN: Thomas Nelson, 2007.

6. Alder, Shannon L. "Good Reads." Web. [http://www.goodreads.com/quotes/457280-i-am-convinced-that-the-jealous-the-angry-the-bitter].

Chapter 2

1. Graham, Billy. "What Christians Want to Know." Web. [http://www.whatchristianswanttoknow.com/20-uplifting-bible-verses-for-times-of-adversity]

2. *Merriam Webster's Collegiate Dictionary, 11th Edition.* Springfield, MA: Merriam-Webster, Inc., 2009.

3. Disney, Walt. "Brainy Quote." Web. [http://www.brainyquote.com/quotes/keywords/adversity.html].

4. "Pharaonic Egypt." Web. [http://www.reshafim.org.il/ad/egypt/timelines/topics/clothing.htm.]

Chapter 3

1. Ford, Henry. "Good Reads." Web. [http://www.goodreads.com/quotes/107178-when-everything-seem-to-be-going-against-you-remember-that].

2. Moore, Beth. *Praying God's Word: Breaking Free from Spiritual Strongholds.* Nashville, TN: B & H Publishing Group, 2009.

Chapter 4

1. Osteen, Joel. *Your Best Life Now: 7 Steps to Living At Your Full Potential.* New York, NY: Warner Faith Time Warner Book Group, 2002.

2. Ancient Hebrew Research Center. "Ancient Hebrew Word Meanings." Web. [http://www.ancient-hebrew.org/27_faith.html].

3. Spurgeon, Charles. *Topics for Today's Living.* Bloomington, IN: Trafford Publishing, 2011.

4. Morris, Robert. *From Dream to Destiny.* Ada, MI: Bethany House Publishers, 2011.

5. Lucado, Max. *The Applause of Heaven.* Nashville, TN: Thomas Nelson, Inc. 1996.

Chapter 5

1. Ortberg, John. *Everybody's Normal Till You Get to Know Them.* Grand Rapids, MI: Zondervan, 2013.

2. Ortberg, John. *If You Want to Walk On Water, You've Got to Get Out of the Boat.* Grand Rapids, MI: Zondervan, 2001.

3. *My Fair Lady,* Director George Cukor, Warner Brothers Entertainment, 1964.

4. Henry, Matthew. *Matthew Henry's Concise Commentary of the Whole Bible.* Nashville, TN: Thomas Nelson, 2003.

5. Rogers, Fred. "Mental Floss." Web. [http://mentalfloss.com/article/31936/20-gentle-quotations-mister-rogers].

Chapter 6

1. Barnes, Roy. "Famous Quotes." Web. [http://www.famousquotesabout.com/on/Tapestry].

2. *Merriam Webster's Collegiate Dictionary, 11th Edition.* Springfield,

MA: Merriam-Webster, Inc., 2009.

3. Ortberg, John. "The Spiritual Life Network." Web. January 15, 2012. [http://life.biblechurch.org/slifejom/process-audio-video/2622-lessons-from-prison-part-2-of-john-ortberg-teaching-on-the-book-unbroken.html].

4. *NIV Quest Study Bible.* Grand Rapids, MI: Zondervan, 2011.

Chapter 7

1. Carr, Robyn. "Family Share." Web. [http://familyshare.com/7-lessons-learned-from-the-bibles-joseph].

Chapter 8

1. Edison, Thomas. "Brainy Quote." Web. [http://www.brainyquote.com/quotes/quotes/t/thomasaed109004.html].

2. Marden, Orison Swett. "Motivational and Inspirational Quotes." Web. [http://www.motivational-inspirational-corner.com/getquote.html].

3. Henry, Matthew. *Matthew Henry's Concise Commentary of the Whole Bible.* Nashville, TN: Thomas Nelson, 2003.

4. Ortberg, John. *The Me I Want to be: Becoming God's Best Version of You.* Grand Rapids, MI: Zondervan, 2010.

Conclusion

1. Tiegreen, Chris. *The One Year Walk with God Devotional: Wisdom from the Bible to Renew Your Mind.* Carol Stream, IL: Tyndale House Publishers, 2004.

2. Tozer, A. W. "Chapel Worship Center." Web. [http://www.chapelworshipcenter.com/sermons/sermons-by-a-w-tozer].